The New Man for Our Time

THE
NEW MAN
FOR
OUR TIME

Elton Trueblood

PROFESSOR-AT-LARGE, EARLHAM COLLEGE

HARPER & ROW, PUBLISHERS

NEW YORK, EVANSTON, AND LONDON

1246

LIBRARY OF CONGRESS CATALOG CARD NUMBER: 77-85059

To
ROBERT PITMAN
Able Colleague

Contents

Preface

THE DECISION to write this book arose when I began to observe the current division within the Christian community described in Chapter I. As I pondered on this, however, my interest broadened until finally my attention was focused upon a larger problem, the problem of how to remain contemporary. This shift began when I realized that one of the inevitable results of exclusive attention to a single aspect of the total gospel is obsolescence.

When we ask seriously how to avoid becoming obsolete, we soon recognize that the good life does not come by the simple-minded effort to restore the past. But with equal clarity we also see that it does not come by any idolatry of what happens to be modern. When human lives have no meaning, they are not saved from their futility by being up-to-date. The man who is wedded to his time will soon be a widower.

As the rate of cultural change accelerates, the problem of how to avoid becoming obsolete increases daily, but the solution of the problem cannot lie in change for the sake of change, since change may mean decline as well as progress. Some deeper level of conviction is required if we are to learn to live well. We have made a start upon our quest when we realize that the art of belonging to one's time is not a matter of language. Few exhibitions are more pathetic than that provided by the person who tries to echo the phrases that he supposes are the newest, but that, in actuality, are already outmoded. It is sad to observe the old who are trying to ape the young in either dress or speech, but who succeed only in sounding ridiculous as they earn the contempt of those whom they seek to flatter by imitation. What makes a difference is not a matter of language but of *ideas*.

Because the one-sided man is inevitably a passing phenomenon, we seek wholeness. In order to endure, a way of life must involve at least three elements: compassion, reverence, and intellectual integrity. The person who is a new man for today, in the sense that he demonstrates this combination, will also be a new man tomorrow. One of my reasons for trying to be a Christian is that the Christian world view comprehends the necessary elements of the good life more fully than does any other body of truth with which I am acquainted. Christianity is a system of life and thought that provides answers to the three basic needs of human beings. This is the reason for the order of chapters in this particular book.

In thinking about this book for many months, and now in writing it, I have had in mind the needs of my readers as I envisage them. I have tried to be sensitive to the many contemporary men and women who, though they have no faith to give meaning to their lives, are sufficiently aware of the spiritual vacuum of the recent past to listen attentively to an affirmative proposal of how life can be made whole. Some of these, I believe, have been rendered sufficiently humble by their own frustrating experiences to understand the paradox that the only way to be truly contemporary is to be more than contemporary.

There is a second group of potential readers to whom I feel very close. These are the people, both lay and clerical, who are experiencing discouragement because the Christian message that they have tried to present to their neighbors has seemed to fall upon deaf ears. Consequently, they recognize keenly the necessity of a new strategy. To the development of such a strategy I have directed my thinking for many years. It is my conviction that Christians have something pertinent to say to the contemporary world and that some are ready to listen.

E. T.

Earlham College
Labor Day, 1969

The New Man for Our Time

I

A Polarized Generation

I would urge that we try to recover in some measure the
horror of divisions among Christians.

WILLIAM TEMPLE

BECAUSE CHRISTIANITY EXISTS, not for its own sake, but for the
sake of the world, all mankind has a stake in the health of the
Christian community. It is the function of the faith to remold
civilization by providing a vision without which the people per-
ish. This service cannot be performed unless the Christian
community demonstrates the unity it seeks to engender. The

15

redemptive process is hindered whenever the faith is fractured.

The sad contemporary truth is that the Christian community is seriously divided. Division is, of course, nothing new; what is new is the form that the division takes. The rift of our generation is not between denominations, which are increasingly similar in faith and in methods of operation. People find it possible to move from one denominational affiliation to another with such remarkable ease that they can hardly tell the difference. Moreover, the once acute conflict between Roman Catholicism and other forms of Christianity is vastly reduced. The employment of national languages in the mass, the practice of using lay readers of the Scriptures, and the growing probability of married clergy all help to bridge the gap that was once so obvious and seemed so hard to cross. But no sooner do we bridge old separations until new ones appear.

The new division that is really serious for the entire Christian Cause is not between denominations, but *within* them. A rift has appeared that runs right down the middle of countless local congregations and is felt in every segment of the total Christian community. The rivalry between sects has been succeeded by the rivalry between parties.

To be truly contemporary is to know where the line of battle is and consequently not waste time and energy upon outworn controversies. Those who are patterning their effort on the battles of the last war are very likely to lose the present one. It is accordingly time to say that anyone who loses sleep over denominational rivalries is really out of touch with his generation and also that anyone who fails to sense the seriousness of the rivalry of parties is equally out of touch. Woe to that person who does not know what time it is! "Why," asked Christ, "do you not know how to interpret the present time?"

(Luke 12:56).[1] While there is a shallow contemporaneity that neglects the rich resources of the past, there is also a profound contemporaneity that makes men seek to concentrate upon those issues that are crucial at the present.

The totality of Christian witness is fractured today because of the emergence of opposing parties, one of which may be called activist and the other pietist. There is no way of knowing what percentages these parties represent, and it would not be helpful to try to assemble figures, but the fact of separation is both undeniable and tragic. In one local church the division has been so sharp, and the consequent bad feeling so great, that seven hundred members have resigned.

By an activist is meant a person who holds that an attack on entrenched social evils is the only part of Christian life that is worth considering. The characteristic activist pickets, organizes marches, signs petitions, and engages in protests. By a pietist, on the other hand, is meant a person who emphasizes the life of prayer, of worship, of devotion, and of personal evangelism. Sometimes he is concerned primarily with the salvation of his own soul, valuing supremely his own peace of mind.

While there have always been both of these emphases in the Christian community, they have, in our generation, become alarmingly sharpened. So sharpened are they, indeed, that many communions have two rival groups looking at each other with mutual suspicion and condescension, each feeling superior to the other. Because some of the most vocal activists are clergymen, the current division appears sometimes to involve clergy on the one side and laymen on the other. The antagon-

[1] Unless otherwise indicated, Scripture quotations are from *The Holy Bible*, Revised Standard Version.

ism is increased by the often suppressed, but always incipient, anticlericalism. Many laymen believe, and even say openly, that the clergy whom they know have departed from the faith. Thus the divisions that were known and often deplored in an earlier generation, the divisions between rival sects and denominations, now seem mild by comparison. The tragedy is that two attitudes, both of which are valuable, have been harmed by mutual isolation. The problem, therefore, is that of a new isolationism.

We understand the Christian crisis better if we realize that the division within the general Christian community is in part a reflection of a division that occurs in the total population. Dag Hammarskjöld was speaking more accurately than he could have known, when in an address at Cambridge University in June, 1960, he said, "The human world is today as never before split into two camps, each of which understands the other as the embodiment of falsehood and itself as the embodiment of truth." We tend to apply these prophetic words to the clash between ideological groupings of nations, but they can be applied, with almost equal appropriateness, to our own citizenry.

The most significant nonreligious division in our nation today is between those who respect and those who reject what, for want of a better term, is called the Protestant ethic. Those who accept this ethic are convinced that a man's personal conduct is important. They honor the paying of debts, fidelity to promises, and an honest day's work. Unfortunately, it is true that some of the people who live and work by this standard have insufficient sympathy for the poor, including those who are on welfare rolls. "I worked to get where I am. Why can't they?" is frequently heard.

On the other side of a deep cultural chasm are the representatives of what some call a new morality. According to this morality, it is primarily concern for the poor and for the ending of war that counts. Accordingly, a man of liberal political tendencies may neglect marital fidelity and yet be pardoned. Some, who are tolerant of infidelity and drunkenness, are not equally tolerant of participation in war. For one part of our population, the key word is honesty; for another part, the key word is compassion.

This gap in our culture is not primarily just a generation gap, as it is not a matter of geography. The contrast is not between urban and rural America; with the wide distribution of television, there is no rural America any more. In some ways, particularly in political division, the parties in question are becoming more isolated from each other, rather than less so. As we read the columns of the commentators, it is often easy to see which of the two ethics is represented. In the light of such a secular division, it is not really very surprising that there should be a serious division in the churches as well.

The social gospel, as preached by Washington Gladden and his associates in the nineteenth century, has been with us a long time. It is in part an application of some of the teachings of Jesus and in part a culmination of the emphasis of the greatest of the prophets of Israel. The present mood was already envisaged by Isaiah when he put stinging words into the mouth of God: "Bring no more vain offerings; incense is an abomination to me" (1:13). The command was to "seek justice, correct oppression; defend the fatherless, plead for the widow" (1:17). No one who knows the Bible at all can fail to be moved both by Micah's searching question of what the Lord requires and by his clear answers. (Mic. 6:8.)[2]

---

[2] "What doth the Lord require of thee, but to do justly, and to love mercy and to walk humbly with thy God?" (av).

What is new today is not the social gospel, but the conviction that the social gospel can stand alone, and that it is the only gospel. Thus it is common to hear participants in Christian conferences say quite frankly that they have no patience with those who waste time on prayer and worship. The idea of a "quiet time" is held by some to be obsolete, because it interferes with possible action and service. The pure activist sometimes expresses open contempt for any who give serious thought to the life of personal devotion, because this seems to him to involve an escape from the urgent business at hand. Why should we read the classics of devotion when workers are needed in organizing the campaign for the allocation of more welfare funds? After all, it is foolish to pay attention to the thoughts of men who lived before the technological age and who cannot give us valid answers because they did not even feel the same problems.

One tangible result of this activist mood has been a lessening of emphasis upon public acts of worship. Some say openly that worship can be omitted without real harm to the Christian Cause and that the loss of Sunday from our culture would not be really damaging, since acts of mercy are possible on every day of the week and in every place. This present emphasis must not be confused with that of the recent past, to the effect that worship one day a week is not sufficient for a full Christian witness and that the crucial test comes in common life. The point of the extreme activist party is not that worship is not *sufficient*, but that it is not even *necessary*. The conviction of some highly articulate leaders today is that the scattered community of service does not need to be undergirded or balanced by the gathered community of devotion. Whereas we used to say that the service begins when the meeting ends, it is now fashionable to say that the meeting can be omitted entirely, without significant loss.

Though it might be argued, theoretically, that a Christianity in which men know how to picket, but not how to pray, is bound to wither, theorizing is not required, because we can already observe the logic of events. The fact is that emphasis upon the life of outer service, without a corresponding emphasis upon the life of devotion, has already led to obviously damaging results, one of which is calculated arrogance. How different it might be if the angry activists were to heed the words found in *The Imitation of Christ*, "Be not angry that you cannot make others as you wish them to be, since you cannot make yourself as you wish to be."[3]

The essence of pietism, by contrast, is the limitation of primary interest to personal salvation. Even today, by the highways, we can see signs paid for by somebody, which urge us to "get right with God." The evil of this well-intentioned effort lies not in what it says, but in what it so evidently omits. The assumption is that salvation is nothing more than a private transaction between the individual and God and that it can become an accomplished, dated event. There are still Christians who do not hesitate to give the exact hour in which personal salvation has occurred. Thus a recent magazine article begins, "I was saved on August 19, 1957."

One of the clearest evidences of our polarized Christian mentality is the choice of hymns. The extreme pietist loves to

[3] *Imitation*, Book I, Chapter 16. This passage is mentioned in Boswell's *Life of Samuel Johnson* under date of 1778. The sentence is a good example of datelessness.

sing, "Near to the Heart of God" and "It is Well with My Soul" while the activist, if he sings any hymns at all, prefers "O Master Let Me Walk with Thee" and "Where Cross the Crowded Ways of Life." In short, one party seeks to express and to celebrate fellowship with God, while the other party is concerned with fellowship with men, especially with those who are unfortunate.

Another concrete evidence of the sharpening polarity is in current religious language. Whereas the normal pietist uses unashamedly the language of devotion, the activist avoids it like a plague. Some clergymen are so afraid of being thought pious that they go even further and engage in ostentatious profanity. They do not seem to realize how transparent such action is, and how similar it is to any adolescent revolt. It is not difficult to see what they are revolting against or that the simplistic pietism being rejected deserves rejection, but the resulting stance misses the mark even further than does the stance being replaced. Ostentatious antipiety is no better than ostentatious piety.

Those who were already in open revolt against pietism felt that they had received strong support when they began to read some of the words that Dietrich Bonhoeffer wrote in Tegel Prison in 1944. What they fastened upon with especial relish was his phrase "religionless Christianity." On the surface, this seemed to uphold the conclusion already reached by many that Christianity divested of the unnecessary baggage of public and private worship could go forward very well. All that would remain, they thought and said, would be confrontation with the world.

The pure activist, who felt that the German martyr had justified such activist conclusions, would have had some healthy misgivings had he thought more deeply. He would have been skeptical about the fairness of adopting uncritically words that were written by a man under severe stress, and without any opportunity of revision before publication. Likewise, he would have matched the isolated quotation with numerous others from the same author, which would have made the conclusion far less simple.

We now have the advantage of a treatment of Bonhoeffer from a careful scholar who has produced the only book about him that has won the approval of his twin sister. "To have discovered in this book," the sister wrote, "a distorted picture of the twin brother to whom I was bound with such powerful ties of affection would have been a bitter grief to me. But this has nowhere been the case."[4] Mary Bosanquet shows convincingly that Bonhoeffer's use of the word "religionless" must be understood in the light of the particular pejorative connotations that the word "religion" happened to have for him. When this is understood, no one who wishes to minimize the life of devotion, in his effort to maximize the life of action, can take any comfort from what the martyr said and did. So far was he from minimizing devotion that in the last view which the prison doctor at Flossenburg had of him, he was kneeling in prayer. His dear friend Eberhard Bethge has made the point in a way hardly to be missed by any thoughtful reader. "The isolated use and handing down of the famous term 'religionless Christianity' has made Bonhoeffer the champion of an undialectical shallow modernism which obscures all that he wanted to tell us about the Living God."[5] When we realize that much

[4] Mary Bosanquet, *The Life and Death of Dietrich Bonhoeffer* (New York: Harper & Row, 1968), Foreword.
[5] *Ibid.*, p. 279.

of the confusion is semantic and no more, we are in a better position to see Bonhoeffer, not as the champion of a party, but as one who sought the wholeness of Christ.

Much of the sadness of the unhappy conflict in the Church arises from the fact that it is unnecessary. It is logically possible to make one emphasis without, at the same time, denying a contrasting one, providing they are not really contradictory. The important observation to make is that the contrasting insights of the activist and the pietist, far from being contradictory, are really complementary. The tragedy is that each party is losing something of essential value that it needs for its own authenticity. The merely active person is not truly active, while the merely devout person is not truly devout. The affirmation of each party is thus ultimately weakened by the character of its denials. Though each part of the total gospel that is stressed is itself a valid one, it loses its validity when it is stressed in isolation, until it finally becomes almost as much an evil as a good. Isolation always involves distortion. In much of our practical life, error is neither patent absurdity nor obvious falsehood; for the most part, it is truth out of context; it is truth in isolation from other truths.

Each party in the present controversy is justified in its criticisms. Thus the evangelical, who is critical of the superficiality of the do-goodism that he observes, is right to criticize, and the service-minded Christian, who is equally critical of inner peace in the midst of human suffering, may, by his criticism, perform a useful service. But if each is willing to end by being critical of opposite extremes, the gain for mankind is negligible. The evangelical may use his resentment at the spectacle of obscenity among protesters to justify his own lack of identification with the improverished and deprived members of the total society. Similarly, the social activist, fearful of sounding pious, may finally undermine the creative center of his own life and thereby lose the motivation for the compassion that he has rightly prized. It is noticeable that many of those who have a compulsive fear of appearing pious, far from being set free, demonstrate a new bondage. Some can no longer engage in vocal prayer, though they may lead a "meditation." They may still be able to talk *about* God, but they cannot talk *to* Him. Thus they are as little emancipated as are the evangelicals who, noting the barrenness of mere social service, reject it as something essentially unworthy. Each party does the same thing: it moves from one gutter to another. Both neglect the ancient wisdom that there is no gain in avoiding one error only to espouse another.

The polarization of our time, which produces half men who could be whole men, may be made vivid by reference to both the roots and the fruits of the Christian faith. The pietist is one who stresses chiefly the roots; the activist is one who stresses chiefly the fruits. Service without devotion is rootless; devotion without service is fruitless. The necessity of stressing each of these without at the same time neglecting the other is abundantly clear in the recorded teaching of Christ Himself. He was certainly presenting the necessity, though not the sufficiency, of human service when He said repeatedly in the Sermon on the Mount, "You will know them by their fruits" (Matt. 7:16, 20). But He was also presenting the balancing truth when He said, "Since it had not root it withered away" (Mark 4:6). Every careful student is well aware of the danger of employing the isolated proof text, because there may be another text that balances and thereby completes it.

The use of paradox in the Gospels is well illustrated by the double emphasis upon deeds and words. On the one hand, Christ said, "Not every one who says to me 'Lord, Lord,' shall enter the kingdom of heaven, but he who does the will of my Father" (Matt. 7:21). On the other hand, the major passage on roots and fruits ends with a sentence highly shocking to modern men, "By your words you will be justified, and by your words you will be condemned" (Matt. 12:37). The pietist, who congratulates himself that his life is Christ-centered, needs to pay attention to the first of these, while the activist who prides himself upon his deeds, needs to pay attention to the second. Of two necessities, neither is the more important. If we neglect the roots, which are found in the life of silent waiting and common prayer, the fruits will soon wither and cease to appear. If we neglect the fruits, which are exhibited in the struggles against injustice, the roots become fundamentally sterile, and the resulting experience is largely self-centered. Indeed, it is possible to bask in a religious experience that, though not sensual, is really another form of self-indulgence.

Any separation between roots and fruits is always damaging. For example, in the campus revolt at Harvard Yard in April, 1969, the leaders of the invasion claimed that they were actuated by compassion for the poor people of Cambridge whose homes were, they said, threatened by the physical growth of the Harvard complex, but this did not keep them from engaging in both words and deeds that were manifestly unloving.[6] On the other side, the person who stresses the roots without the fruits may indulge in a heart-warming experience, unconcerned about the poor housing of many of his neighbors.

The Christian division of our generation may be expressed

[6] *Harvard Today*, Spring, 1969.

in several different ways. One way is to point out the contrast between those who are devotion-centered and those who are service-centered. Each finds it easy to criticize the other because each is vulnerable. The service-centered Christian is vulnerable because the service that he prides himself on performing often descends into the impersonalism of the welfare office, with the fire of compassion burning low because it is not refueled from within. The devotion-centered person is vulnerable because, in his concentration upon the love of Christ, he may easily forget those whom Christ loves. Judgment of others is therefore easy, but also dangerous, for one is as vulnerable as the other. Christ's message on judgment is particularly significant now because we live in a judgmental age, when nearly every protest is couched in harsh terms, unqualified condemnation being the order of the day. But the trouble with judgment is that it is always a potential boomerang. It is a mistake to suppose that the Christian must never judge; that Christ judged the Pharisees is obvious.

The essence of Christ's teaching about judgment is not that He forbade it, but that He made clear what its implications are. If you don't want to be criticized, don't criticize, but of course you must, unless you opt for mindless tolerance. The crucial words, therefore, are to the effect that every judgment involves a self-judgment. "For with the judgment you pronounce you will be judged" (Matt. 7:2). Every activist who criticizes the pietist for presenting less than the whole gospel should examine his own stance and vice versa.

The late Paul Tillich helped to achieve a fresh look at the important question of judgment when he called attention to the fact that Christ judged and that understanding does not replace judging. "The sinners," he pointed out in a famous sermon, "one a whore and the other a companion of whores, are not excused by ethical arguments which remove the seriousness of the moral demand. They are not excused by sociological explanations which would remove their personal responsibility."[7] The new man for our age, whom Professor Tillich envisioned, especially in his eloquent preaching, was one who could be tough while he was tender. The picture is of a person who refuses to settle for either permissiveness or violence, and who is not overimpressed by the particular idols of his particular age. When other aspects of Tillich's theology have been forgotten, his emphasis upon the new kind of person may be remembered with gratitude.

One obvious fragmentation of the total gospel is represented by the supposed necessity of choosing between the needs of the individual and the needs of society. Those who emphasize the individual point out quite rightly that it is really the individual who makes a difference in the sequence of historical events. Whenever something big occurs, they say, it is reasonable to look for a *man*. If one man such as John R. Mott is converted, he will, in consequence, influence the lives of countless others and thereby leave an enduring impact, for history is altered when a person finds a new center of his life. Changes in society, it is truly stated, come primarily because of changes in men. Every true revolution begins, not in some abstraction called society, but in some man's heart. The best college is not the one with the newest curriculum, but the one with the ablest teachers. The Church is, at best, not an efficient hierarchy, but an incendiary fellowship, and it is individual men who start the fires. St. Augustine was accurate when he portrayed the entire Christian enterprise as that in which one loving heart

---

[7] *The New Being* (New York: Charles Scribner's Sons, 1955), p. 4.

sets another on fire. Friends of George Buttrick have often heard him say, "If religion does not begin with the individual, it never begins; but if it ends with the individual—it ends!" This is the double truth that the interpreters of the gospel need to emphasize tirelessly in all situations.

More common than individual salvation is the stress today on social reconstruction. Those who do so point out quite rightly that it is very difficult to become new persons in the throes of deep poverty, crowding, and unemployment. They admit that Abraham Lincoln flowered in the poverty and severe hardship of the Pigeon Creek neighborhood of southern Indiana, but they think of this as an exception, and doubt if the experience can be repeated in the midst of contemporary urban poverty. Consequently, they say that it is idle to try to introduce a man of the slums to Jesus Christ. First, it is necessary to remove the constant temptation to drug addiction and to help people to engage in the kind of industry that will enable them to be self-respecting. To speak to a hungry man of Christ, it is frequently said, is to insult him.

Modest as the word appears to be, one of the greatest of all Christian terms is the word "and." We have the beneficent example of Christ Himself who used this conjunction conspicuously in connection with the competing claims of the old and the new. "Every scribe," He said, "who has been trained for the kingdom of heaven is like a householder who brings out of his treasure what is new and what is old" (Matt. 13:52). Herein lies a vivid rebuke both to the one who pines for the good old days and to the one who has contempt for anything that is not strictly contemporary.

The revolutionary and truly contemporary message is that choice is not always required, the pressures of the age notwithstanding. It is a mistake, for example, to suppose that we must choose between being liberals and being conservatives, inasmuch as every sound person is something of both. Everyone who is intellectually and spiritually alive is a liberal, in the sense that he is open to truth from any quarter, welcoming any evidence without the bondage of prejudgment. Similarly, each person who thinks with any care is a conservative, partly because he is unwilling to waste whatever has proved itself in the long experience of history, and partly because he knows that the most recent emphasis is not automatically the most wise. It is conceivable that at any particular juncture in history, it may be right and good to emphasize one or the other side of the liberal-conservative totality, because immediate needs demand such emphasis, but no really wise man will ever settle permanently for either one alone. The thinking involved in the use of "and" is far more profound than that involved in the employment of "either-or."

Is the Christian a person who loves God, or is he one who loves his fellow men? Though the question is asked, it is really a foolish one. A Christian is one who is committed to Christ, and Christ stressed the two commandments without preference. Though there are many paradoxes in the Gospels, and though its truth cannot be rightly stated apart from paradox, there is no paradox more striking than that of the "double priority." Christ gave two "firsts." The one "first" was exactly what His hearers expected, because they were familiar with the Shema (Deut. 6:4), which was repeated daily. They knew that they were required to love God and to love Him wholly.

The other "first," which in the teaching of Christ is of equal standing, is the requirement that the disciple should love his neighbor *as himself* (Lev. 19:18). The Christian, accordingly, is convinced that there can be no adequate faith that does not recognize and encourage this double priority. A Christian is asked to include in his life both piety and service. Then he can hold the roots and the fruits of the faith in one organic context. Each needs the other.

Some of the current Roman Catholic thinkers and writers, who face exactly the same division as that in Protestant congregations, are potentially helpful by their insistence upon the necessity of holding together the twin concepts of Father and Brother. "It is only when we are subject to a common father that we are brothers," says Louis Everly. "To become brothers we have only to become sons again."[8] The man who really believes in God can see another human being as an object of infinite value, while the one who truly loves other humans has the necessary depth of emotion in his life to enable him to begin his encounter with the Father.

It is important to affirm that every genuine follower of Christ is both catholic and protestant in his mentality, regardless of his official membership. He is necessarily catholic because he experiences unity, even though union may not be possible or even wise. He is, at the same time, necessarily protestant because he must hold sacred the personal Christian experience, regardless of what any hierarchy may say. What we dare never relinquish is the bold conception that the two sides of this Christian totality can be kept together in any one life and that, furthermore, each needs the other for its own fulfillment.

Human nature does not change and God does not change, but human philosophies change precisely because they are human. These philosophies make a great difference in the

[8] *We Dare to Say Our Father* (New York: Herder and Herder, 1967), p. 9.

course of events, a false philosophy having vast and evil consequences. This is why Christians, if they are to take a genuine lead in their generation in producing the new mentality so sorely needed, must be critical of all thinking which polarizes men. When we examine the situation carefully, we realize that many of our uncritically accepted classifications do nothing but harm. Why, for example, should Christian men be classified as rational or evangelical when it is obvious that all who seek to follow Christ deserve both appellations? A serious Christian is a rationalist because he knows that he must be able to present a reason for the hope that is in him (I Pet. 3:15), but he likewise knows that he must enter the kingdom like a child (Mark 10:15). Why should a man be required to choose between the traditional and the contemporary? Unless he is completely confused by the cries of the present, he is humble enough to learn from wise men of other centuries. If he were forced to choose between Pascal's *Pensées* and the latest bestseller, he would probably learn more from the former than from the latter. But since, at the same time, he is deeply concerned about modern life, he must seek to know God's will for today. Though he is willing to learn from other generations, and realizes that he has much to learn, it is the modern application that interests him most, for no thoughtful person can have a merely inherited faith. What is really foolish is the supposition that there is some inherent conflict between the willingness to learn from the past and the urgency to live well in the present.

The new man for our time is the whole man, the man who consciously rejects the temptation to limit himself to one part of a totality, when such limitation is not required. But where is the inspiration to wholeness to be found? It is certainly not found in our current political operations, and seldom is it found in science. The truth is that it is most likely to be found in the Christian faith. Though it is sorrowfully true that some of the worst fragmentation is currently demonstrated in the Christian community itself, the Christian faith, particularly through its Founder and its Scriptures, possesses resources for the transcendence of one-sidedness. By the miracle of the preservation of the Gospels, Christians have a marvelous antidote to divisiveness of every kind. If they will study the Gospels directly, and not merely study *about* them, they will find in them the fairest presentation of wholeness that the human race has known. There is found One who weeps and One who laughs, and only the foolish suppose that there is any incompatibility between these two expressions of the divine character. There is found equal emphasis upon the life of devotion and the life of action. Only the obtuse can fail to see that Christ both healed and prayed, and that in His judgment the former could not be achieved without the latter (Mark 9:29).

What is becoming increasingly clear is that the major tragedy of the new separatism emerges because each party is deprived of something that it needs, and something that the opposite party has to offer. The pietist needs action and the activist needs piety. Each is a half man, made such by an unnecessary act of self-limitation and consequent impoverishment. The really wonderful fact is that a number of Christian leaders are now keenly aware of this, and are, consequently, trying to develop the new image that the life of our times requires. The best leaders are both service-centered and Christ-centered.

It is time now to take a further step and to show that the new man who is to be truly contemporary must include, not just two, but three elements in the totality of his faith. These

three are like three legs of a stool, the smallest number possible
if the stool is to stand upright. The three necessary elements
in any genuine Christianity are, first, the experience of inner
vitality that comes by the life of prayer, second, the experience
of outer action in which the Christian carries on a healing
ministry, both to individuals and to social institutions, and
third, the experience of careful thinking by which the credibility of the entire operation may be supported. Religions tend
to die when any one of the three is omitted for an extended
period of time.

When this book was first contemplated, it was thought that
it might be called "The Roots and the Fruits," with equal
stress on unashamed piety and compassionate service. But as
the idea grew in the author's mind, it became increasingly clear
that, because more is required, the twofold title would be both
inappropriate and inaccurate. We must, indeed, cultivate the
roots, if anything is to grow, and we must exhibit the fruits
of service if our devotion is to be genuine, but these together
will not suffice. We must also be able to think with such clarity
that we cut through the fog of confusion. Who is more likely
to be able to do this than the committed Christian? Far from
indulging in wish-thinking, he knows that he cannot be a faithful recruit in Christ's Cause unless he is truly tough-minded.
He is as eager as is any scientist to reject any unverified hy-
pothesis because, as he tries to follow Christ, he knows that he is
dealing with God's truth, which is intrinsically sacred. No
matter how invigorating prayer may be, it will eventually come
to an end if it does not fit into a pattern of truth about the
world that makes sense. The religions of ancient Greece died,
not only because they were socially irrelevant, but also because,
for thoughtful persons, they were no longer believable. If the

Christian view of the world is not true, and if people discover that it is not true, it will not endure. If it cannot meet the most searching intellectual inquiry, prayer will cease because it will be rightly seen as a form of self-hypnosis, and Christian social action will, accordingly, lose its central motivation.

The vocation of the Christian is threefold: he is called to *pray*, to *serve*, and to *think*, and he is called to do all three together. If he can be faithful to this calling, he will provide something really new in our generation. Though there are numerous persons who are attempting one of these three, those who attempt all three at once are living on a genuine frontier. The best thing we can do for our troubled world is to increase the number who, because they are committed to the threefold pattern, are the genuinely new men of our time.

II

A Demonstration of Wholeness

Only connect.

E. M. FORSTER

ONCE WE KNOW with some accuracy what the real divisions of the Christian community are, we are in a better position to try to heal them. Realizing that we dare not remain satisfied with emphasis on only one side of what is really indivisible, we must employ the best thought that we can muster, to avoid the polarization that is uniformly debilitating. We soon see that the answer does not lie in compromise, but rather in combination. We seek a mean, but it is a mean of comprehension. The effective politician is not the one who operates halfway between liberalism and conservativism, but the one who is able to combine the valuable elements of both of these in his approach to specific problems.

Much of the answer to polarization is to be found in a new conception of ecumenicity. What is required in this conception is not church union, which may or may not develop, but a new understanding of the meaning of "and." The combination we seek is that which unites the different aspects of an individual's faith. Important as unity in the churches may be, the unity of individual lives is still more important, because it is prior. We seek a unity both of tense and of mood.

It is necessary to see clearly that it is a mistake to place exclusive trust in the experience of the present, just as it is a mistake to trust only the past. The person who is concerned only with what is gone is hardly alive, while the person who is concerned with only the present has a life empty of content. Since the facts that we know by memory, or by the reports of those whom we have reason to trust, vastly outnumber those that we know by immediate experience, unwillingness to learn from earlier experience simply means intellectual and spiritual impoverishment. If we reject ideas from an earlier century *because* they are earlier, we are logically driven to reject those of the past year, the past day, and even the past hour. This is where the doctrine of bare contemporaneity would lead, if those who profess it were to be sincere, and should be honest enough to accept the logical implications of their basic proposition. They would be as shallow as the Athenians and foreigners who, at the time of the Apostle Paul's visit to Athens, "spent their time in nothing except telling or hearing something new" (Acts 17:21).

The same is true of the need for both reason and passion. The man of reason, devoid of passion, becomes bloodless, while the man of passion, devoid of reason, has no way of resisting the appeal of any dogma or even of any superstition. The lessons of history are replete with this double truth. The only person who is able to operate effectively in our complex age is one who recognizes that there is no incompatibility between the warm heart and the clear head. The new Christian man, who can give leadership for the new day, is the one who, without even a hint of contradiction, can enjoy studying the works of Aristotle and, on the same day, appreciate singing "Jesus, Lover of My Soul." The worst mark of confusion is the prejudice that a man cannot do both. Those who demonstrate, without apology or undue self-consciousness, that they *can* do both, will be respected and followed. They will be able to make something of the impact upon our time that William Temple made upon his, when his characteristic titles were *Christus Veritas* and *Mens Creatrix*.

The combination represented by the evangelical Anglican is so effective and so appealing that we might reasonably expect its wide adoption. A Christian leader of this character is effective precisely because he is able to make the best of both worlds. He demonstrates, for all to see, that William James was wrong in his facile acceptance of the idea that people must be either tough-minded or tender-minded. The really effective leaders are both, and they are both at once.

The combination of tough-mindedness and deep devotion that Thomas Carlyle admired in his father set the standard of his own brilliant career. Those who have read Carlyle's moving essay on his father are not likely to forget the line, "He was religious with the consent of his whole faculties." The paragraph in which this sentence appears is so apposite to our time that it justifies full quotation.

My father's education was altogether of the worst and most limited. I believe he was never more than three months at any school. What he learned there showed what he might have learned. A solid knowledge of arithmetic, a fine antique handwriting—these with other limited practical etceteras, were all the things he ever heard mentioned as excellent. He had no room to strive for more. Poetry, fiction in general, he had universally seen treated as not only idle, but false and criminal. This was the spiritual element he had lived in, almost to old age. But greatly his most important culture he had gathered—and this, too, by his own endeavours—from the better part of the district, the religious men; to whom, as to the most excellent, his own nature gradually attached and attracted him. He was religious with the consent of his whole faculties. Without religion he would have been nothing. Indeed, his habit of intellect was thoroughly free, and even incredulous. And strongly enough did the daily example of this work afterwards on me. . . . Religion was the pole-star for my father. Rude and uncultivated as he otherwise was, it made him and kept him "in all points a man."[1]

Shall we stress words or deeds? Insofar as we are Christians we shall stress both. The popular pose of those who claim that words are not needed, because deeds are everything, have missed the important point that the best deeds *are* words. Frequently, the words that we are able to say to a distraught or confused person help that person most. What you remember most gratefully may be something that someone *said* to you

[1] Thomas Carlyle, *Reminiscences* (New York: Charles Scribner's Sons, 1881), p. 16. The essay on James Carlyle was written in 1832, soon after his death.

long ago. It is not enough to give a cup of cold water; it is necessary also to tell *why*.

One of the best reasons for a practical ecumenicity is not the elimination of different emphases in the Christian faith, which might entail a genuine loss to the total Christian Cause, but rather the encouragement of sharing that which will complement and thereby enrich. It is far better to be both an intellectual and an evangelical than to be either one alone. Contrast need not mean incompatibility.

The patent failure of the secularized college is a vivid demonstration of the mistake of emphasizing only one part of the total gospel. It is right that a college should be secular in that it should operate in the world and for the world. There is, accordingly, little defense for a private institution that exists primarily for the sake of a particular party or denomination, but there is a very strong defense for an institution that is independent in support, while it is public in responsibility. What is increasingly obvious is that the plight of the ex-Christian college is a really deplorable one. Once the commitment to Christ is rejected or forgotten, such an institution, lacking the strength of the state institutions, becomes nondescript. As long as the Christian college maintains its vision of wholeness, it is often a place of tremendous hope in the creation of a civilization, but its major effectiveness ends when the wholeness ends. Its greatness declines when it ceases to hold the love of God and the love of learning in a single context.

As we seek to facilitate the emergence of a new pattern of human life that combines, equally, the inner and the outer life, maintaining both the roots of vitality and the fruits of service, we are helped by concentrating our attention upon individuals who, in any generation, have demonstrated such a pattern.

Indeed, demonstration is far better for our present purposes than speculation, because speculation is unverified. After all, the best that we ever encounter is not a good system or a good doctrine, but a good person. A really good man is the most wonderful item in all creation, far superior to any machine, any book, or any work of nature.

Fortunately, our generation has had some striking examples of personal wholeness. One such was Rufus M. Jones (1863-1948), who taught philosophy at Haverford College for forty productive years until his retirement in 1934. Though he earned his living as a teacher of philosophy, Rufus M. Jones was not willing to settle for this alone. His time was largely given to public service, especially as chairman of the American Friends Service Committee, in which capacity he had much to do with healing the wounds of war. Along with work of the mind and social service, Dr. Jones kept up a heavy schedule of preaching all over the world, especially in college chapels, told remarkably funny stories, cultivated countless friendships, and nurtured a deep life of devotion. He was more sure, he said, of the presence of God than of the presence of any human being. The widely differing aspects of his career never seemed to be in conflict, but always seemed to strengthen each other.

There are, of course, other exemplars of such wholeness, each thoughtful reader of these pages having his own prized examples. Much of the appeal of Albert Schweitzer arises because this famous man required of himself that he be both an intellectual and *more* than an intellectual. Our own lives have been dignified by being contemporaries of a man who combined philosophy, theology, music, and medicine, and who excelled in the practice of all four of these. Recently we have had the rich experience of encountering Dr. Schweitzer in another role, that of preacher, for some of his sermons were fortunately preserved in shorthand.[2] Always the advice is that of refusing to settle for littleness or partiality when magnitude is possible.

Among those who have demonstrated the Christian pattern of wholeness, one of the most outstanding is John Woolman (1720-1772). Where others are eminent, Woolman is a giant. More than one hundred years before the Civil War, this simple-hearted man inaugurated an effective plan of immediate emancipation of slaves in America, while at the same time he wrote his *Journal* in such an attractive fashion that it has become a devotional classic.

The essence of Woolman's story, profound as it is, may be quickly told. Born in the village of Rancocas, New Jersey, Woolman enjoyed a modest education and settled, as a young man, in Mt. Holly. He was an affectionate husband and father and a respected citizen of his community. He soon came to be self-employed as a tailor, his work involving also that of a small business establishment. Very early, as his business began to prosper, this unique man, fearing that money-making might take too much of his time, urged his customers to patronize his competitors. Keenly aware of the dangers of affluence, he determined to keep his way of life as simple as was possible, and, for awhile, even wore undyed clothing. Partial freedom from business allowed him time to travel widely in the itinerant ministry, his most important visits being two to Virginia and North Carolina, one to the Indians on the Susquehanna River, and a final visit to England where he died of smallpox. His body is buried in York.

The effectiveness of Woolman and others who joined him

[2] Albert Schweitzer, *Reverence for Life* (New York: Harper & Row, 1969).

in the effort to eradicate slavery was greater than even Woolman anticipated. Only four years after his death, the religious body to which he belonged forbade the ownership of slaves among its members, while the entire slave system was abolished by law in Pennsylvania in 1780, and in New Jersey in 1803. Crucial to much of this development was an address made by Woolman in 1758. That so mild a man could make so much difference is one of the surprises of history.

Woolman's literary production includes, besides his *Journal*, the following short books and essays, most of which are concerned with the social application of a vital Christian faith:

Some Considerations on the Keeping of Negroes, Part I, 1754, and Part II, 1762.

A Plea for the Poor, 1763.

Considerations on the True Harmony of Mankind, 1770.

Last Essays. Written at Sea and in England, 1773.

The *Journal* was already sufficiently admired and established only twenty-five years after Woolman's death to make Charles Lamb speak of it with deep respect. On February 5, 1797, Lamb wrote to his friend Coleridge, "[Charles] Lloyd has kindly left me for a keep-sake, *John Woolman*. You have read it, he says, and like it. Will you excuse one short extract? I think it could not have escaped you:—'Small treasure to a resigned mind is sufficient. How happy is it to be content with a little, to live in humility, to feel *that* in us which breathes out this language—Abba! Father!'" As Lamb went on reading the *Journal* and also some of the shorter productions of Woolman's mind, the impression deepened until, in 1822, he wrote the much-quoted laconic sentence: "Get the Writings of John Woolman by heart." The chain of influence which connects

Woolman, Lamb's *Essays of Elia,* and countless subsequent readers is good to contemplate. The chain is still intact.[3]

Sensitive readers soon begin to see why Lamb made such a strong recommendation of the writings of an unpretentious man when they note the remarkable combination that Woolman's experience represents. On the one hand, they make the acquaintance of a man who was humbly and unapologetically devout, while, on the other hand, he was clearly an activist. During the last day of his life, he called for pen and ink and wrote, with much difficulty, his final message as follows: "I believe my being here is in the wisdom of Christ; I know not as to life or death." From beginning to end, the devout man sought to live in the divine presence and to seek a wisdom not his own.

A good example of Woolman's combination of social concern and personal obedience to the divine leading is provided by one of his visits to a part of Carolina where there were many slaves. Though he could be eloquent and persuasive in the public ministry, Woolman sought consistently not to run ahead of his Guide. Consequently, he did not always speak. At Wells Creek, in May, 1757, he could report that "the Gospel Ministry was opened and the Love of Jesus Christ experienced amongst us, to his name be the praise." But, iniquitous as slavery appeared to him to be, the gentle messenger kept silent on that subject. The following passage from the *Journal* explains his practice of abstinence from words:

[3] The best way to encounter John Woolman is through the Rancocas Edition of *The Journal and Essays of John Woolman* edited, with a biographical introduction, by Amelia Mott Gummere (New York: The Macmillan Company, 1922). Those for whom Mrs. Gummere's fine edition is unavailable will find shorter versions profitable. The best of these is the Everyman Edition.

As the Neglected Condition of the poor Slaves often Affects my mind, Meetings for Discipline hath seem'd to me Sutable places to Express what the Holy Spirit may open on that Subject, and though in this meeting they were much in my mind, I found no Engagement to speak concerning them, and therefore kept Silence, finding by Experience that to keep pace with the gentle Motions of Truth, and never move but as That Opens the way, is necessary for the true Servant of Christ.[4]

In the next settlement that he visited, Woolman's mind, he said, "was deeply Exercised concerning the poor Slaves," but, in spite of this, he did not feel free to speak. "I was bowed in spirit before the Lord," he wrote, "and with tears and inward supplication besought him, to open my understanding, that I might know his will concerning me, and at length, my mind was settled in Silence." Though this might appear to be a cowardly rejection of confrontation, such was not the case, and the inner control turned out to be remarkably effective. So effective was it that by the end of the century, more than sixty years before the Civil War, all of the Quakers of North and South Carolina had emancipated their once numerous slaves.

Woolman was demonstrating, in regard to human slavery, what may rightly be termed a "third way." On the one hand, he did not settle for the kind of piety in which he would have been primarily concerned with his own salvation, yet, on the other, he refused to indulge in violent denunciation of the slaveowners. Though slavery was recognized as an evil, the persons who were engaged in it were not personally attacked; they were approached without the reformer indulging in the psychic pay-off which comes so easily by concentrating upon an injustice which allows him to indulge freely his own rage

[4] *Journal*, Rancocas Edition, p. 199.

and hatred. Woolman was too conscious of his own failings to start screaming at others in self-righteous indignation. Though he knew that he had discovered a valid cause, his life was too rich to be simplistic, even about the cause to which he was devoted. The slaves, he saw, were persons made in God's image, but the owners were persons too.

Woolman began to feel, on his first southern journey at the age of twenty-six, a serious problem about hospitality. He did not want to seem ungrateful or rude to his hosts, yet at the same time he could not, with consistency, allow himself to profit, in personal comfort, from an iniquitous system. To share the benefits was, in one sense, to condone! "When I eat drank and lodged free cost with people who lived in Ease in the hard toyle of their slaves," he wrote, "I feel uneasie."[5] The inconsistency of seeming to condone slavery by his own conduct, though opposing it by public speech, deeply bothered him, because, as he said, "Conduct is more convincing than language." He was most explicit when he wrote the following sentence: "As it is common for Friends on a visit to have Entertainment free cost, a difficulty arose in my mind with respect to saveing my own money by kindness received, which to me appeared to be the gain of Opression."[6]

Woolman's solution of the problem of hospitality where slaves were involved is illustrated by what occurred at London Grove, Pennsylvania, November 18, 1758. After Woolman had delivered a powerful sermon against slavery, he went, with others, to the home of Thomas Woodward for dinner. Upon entering the house of his host, Woolman observed some Negro servants and soon learned that they were slaves. With no re-

[5] *Ibid.*, p. 167.
[6] *Ibid.*, p. 188.

monstrance, and without a word of any kind, he quietly left the house. When the guests assembled at the dinner table, all soon realizing the reason for Woolman's absence, the effect on the plantation owner was more powerful than a direct rebuke could have been. On waking the next morning, Thomas Woodward told his wife that they must liberate their slaves. Though his wife burst into tears at the thought of losing her faithful helpers in the kitchen, the husband went through with the decision. *He was unwilling to maintain the kind of household in which a man as good as John Woolman did not feel free to be entertained.* As a further consequence of this tender yet powerful form of social protest, Thomas Woodward became involved in the antislavery movement. Only two years later the religious body to which the Quaker of London Grove belonged passed a minute that said, "The growing concern, which hath appeared amongst us for some years past, to discourage the Practice of making Slaves of our Fellow Creatures, hath been visibly blest with Success."[7]

When contemporary Christians assume, as they often do, that it is necessary to choose between tenderness and toughness, they are helped by knowing that in such a man as John Woolman, these could be combined and that the combination could be effective. Woolman engaged in protest, but did not, by so doing, alienate those against whose actions he was protesting.

The important lesson that Woolman provides for modern man lies not in the fact that he stressed equally the life of devotion and the life of social consciousness, remarkable as

[7] Epistle (broadside) from Yearly Meeting held at Burlington, 9 mo. 27, 1760, signed by John Smith, Clerk. The broadside is deposited in the Haverford College Library.

that is, but rather the particular way in which the one actually led to the other. Woolman's social consciousness, concerning both the poor and the enslaved, arose, not in spite of, but *because* of his rich life of devotion. It was when he meditated deeply upon the universal love of God that he realized that each person has a moral responsibility to help all creatures to share in that love, without man-made limitations. All that we own, therefore, we own in the light of "a common interest from which our own is inseparable." We are brothers because we derive from a common Father. Our genuine vocation is to become God's instruments in the liberation of all. This profound conception led him to say, in a now-famous expression, that "to turn all the treasures we possess into the Channel of Universal Love, becomes the business of our lives."[8]

After Woolman's return to New Jersey, following his first southern journey, he wrote, at the surprisingly young age of twenty-six, his first manuscript dealing with slavery. The manuscript reflects a mature understanding of the fact that love is not sufficient, because it may be the wrong kind of love. "In our present Condition," the young man wrote, "to *Love* our Children is needful; but except this *Love* proceeds from the true heavenly Principle which sees beyond earthly treasures, it will rather be injurious than of any real Advantage to them: where the Fountain is corrupt, the Streams must necessarily be impure."[9] The only love that Woolman really trusted was that which springs from the love of God.

It was primarily a meditation upon a Biblical passage that seems, in the first instance, to have alerted Woolman's clear mind to the fact that a human institution, long accepted uncrit-

[8] "A Plea for the Poor," Chap. III, *Journal, op. cit.*, p. 405.
[9] *Journal*, p. 335.

ically, was actually an evil one. The passage that started him on his moral journey was that of Genesis 3:20, "And Adam called his wife's name Eve, because she was the mother of all living." Here the important insight was that if Eve was the mother of all, then all people of all races are truly "of one blood." This is bound to include people brought from Africa, in precisely the same sense that it includes all who came from Europe. The fact that the latter came voluntarily, while the former came under compulsion, has no bearing whatever on the universality of the heritage. In a particularly revealing passage, Woolman pointed out the consequence of his major insight, to the effect "that in this World we are but Sojourners, that we are subject to the like Afflictions and Infirmities of Body, the like Disorders and Frailties of Mind, the like Temptations, the same Death, and the same Judgment, and that the Alwise Being is Judge and Lord over us all."[10]

Once there is recognized the same ancestry and the same fundamental human condition, uniting both freemen and slaves, "it seems to raise an Idea of a general Brotherhood, and a disposition easy to be touched with a Feeling of each other's Afflictions." As Woolman prayed and meditated, the burden of the world's suffering lay upon him. This burden caused him to worry about his country, because he saw that the consequences of uncorrected injustice would someday be terrible. In 1746, one hundred fifteen years before the start of the Civil War, he predicted a sorrowful outcome of the sin of slavery. "I saw," he wrote, "so many Vices and Corruptions increased by this trade and this way of life, that it appeared to me as a dark gloominess hanging over the Land, and though now

[10] *Ibid.*, p. 337.

many willingly run into it, yet in future the Consequence will be grievous to posterity."[11] Some developments of the last third of the twentieth century constitute as much a verification of Woolman's insight into the working of the moral law as did the Civil War itself.

Woolman's vision of a dark gloominess hanging over the land, which was really a vision of human suffering, was given its most vivid expression when he was ill with pleurisy in 1770. Two years later, shortly before his death in England, Woolman recalled his dream for insertion in his *Journal*. This, with its interpretation, has come to be recognized as one of the classic statements of religious experience, not greatly different from that of John Donne when he realized that the bell was tolling for him. It is part of the life of devotion, and it is also productive of social action. The important passage is:

I was brought so Near the gates of death, that I forgot my name. Being then desirous to know who I was, I saw a mass of matter of a dull gloomy collour, between the South and the East, and was informed that this mass was human beings, in as great misery as they could be, & live, and that I was mixed in with them, & henceforth I might not consider myself as a distinct or Separate being. In this state I remained several hours. I then heard a soft melodious voice, more pure and harmonious than any voice I had heard with my ears before, and I believed it was the voice of an angel who spake to the other angels. The words were *John Woolman is dead*. I soon remembered that I once was John Woolman, and being assured that I was alive in the body, I greatly wondered what that heavenly voice could mean.

I believed beyond doubting that it was the voice of an holy Angel, but as yet it was a mystery to me.

I was then carried in Spirit to the mines, where poor Oppressed

11 *Ibid.*, p. 167.

people were digging rich treasures for those called Christians, and heard them blaspheme the name of Christ, at which I was grieved for his Name to me was precious.

Then I was informed that these heathen were told that those who oppressed them were the followers of Christ; and they said amongst themselves, If Christ directed them to use us in this Sort then Christ is a cruel tyrant.

All this time the song of the Angel remained a Mystery, and in the morning my dear wife and some others coming to my bedside I asked them if they knew who I was, and they telling me I was John Woolman, thought I was only light-headed, for I told them not what the Angel said, nor was I disposed to talk much to any one; but was very desirous to get so deep that I might understand this Mystery.

My tongue was often so dry that I could not speak till I had moved it about and gathered some moisture, and as I lay still for a time, at length I felt divine power prepare my mouth that I could speak, and then I said, "I am crucified with Christ, nevertheless I live yet not I, but Christ [that] liveth in me, and the life I now live in the flesh is by faith [in] the Son of God who loved me and gave himself for me."

Then the Mystery was opened and I perceived there was Joy in heaven over a Sinner who had repented, and that that language, *John Woolman is dead*, meant no more than the death of my own will.[12]

The more closely Woolman identified his life with the life and love of Christ, the more he became sensitive to suffering. Thus, on his one and only voyage to England, he was naturally expected to go first class on the ship *Mary and Elizabeth*, because his companion, Samuel Emlen, had already taken passage in the cabin. But when Woolman saw the difference in treatment of the classes, he made his witness for solidarity with the less privileged by taking passage in the steerage. This, like many

[12] *Ibid.,* pp. 308-9.

decisions involving the social order, came after much prayer and serious consideration, because to him the choice was not a trivial one. On the one hand, he was not physically strong, and his friends laid before him the great inconvenience of steerage quarters. On the other hand, he had strong scruples about excessive comfort when this was possible for only a few. "My mind," he said, "was turned toward Christ, the heavenly Counsellor; & I feeling at this time my own will subjected, my heart was contrite before [him]." His explanation of his final decision was as follows:

I told the owner that I had at Several times in my travels, seen great oppression on this continent at which my heart had been much affected, and brought often into a feeling of the state of the Sufferers. And having many times been engaged, in the fear and love of God, to labour with those under whom the oppressed have been born down and afflicted, I have often perceived that [it was with] a view to get riches, and provide estates for Children to live conformable to customs, which stand in that Spirit wherein men have regard to the honours of this world. That in the pursuit of these things, I had seen many entangled in the Spirit of oppression and the exercise of my Soul had been such, that I could not find peace in joining with any thing which I saw was against that wisdom which is pure.

If there is any better example in all religious literature of the combination of personal devotion and social witness, we do not know where it is to be found. In practice the human service that emerged from the prayerful decision was considerable. Woolman's life for many days in cramped quarters gave him, he reported, "sundry opportunities of seeing, hearing and feeling" the life of many of the sailors. "I being much amongst the Sea men, have from a motion of love, sundry times taken opportunities with one alone, and in a free conversation, laboured to turn their heads toward the fear of the Lord." Later he said, "I often feel a tenderness of heart toward these poor lads, and at times, look at them as though they were my Children according to the flesh."[13]

Woolman's sensitivity to suffering included not only the various members of the human race, but all of God's creatures. This sensitivity caused him, on his English journey, to do something that seemed, to many, singular or even quixotic. Noting that the stage coaches were able to keep to their schedules over bad roads only by overworking the horses, he decided to walk from London to York. By the route that he chose, this walking journey was of at least 400 miles. He was also influenced by the suffering of the boys who were employed in handling horses and coaches. "Stage Coaches," he reported, "frequently go upwards of a hundred miles in 24 hours, and I have heard friends say, in several places, that it is common for horses to be killed with hard driving, and many others are driven till they go blind."[14] The tender man was well aware that he was personally unable to stop a practice that troubled him, but he also knew that he could at least refuse to profit by it. Not only did Woolman refuse to ride; he also refused to make use of the coaches in sending letters, even cautioning friends not to send letters to him "on any common occasion by post."

The probability is that Woolman's self-denial, arising out of his deep sensitivity to the suffering of his fellow creatures, hastened his own death. When he was stricken with smallpox in York, he was well attended by his English hosts, but the journey had weakened him and the man often mentioned as

13 *Ibid.*, pp. 289-292.
14 *Ibid.*, p. 306.

the one authentic American saint died at the too early age of fifty-two. He died, as he lived, in the effort to watch diligently against "the motions of self" in his own mind. He even gave attention to the simple burial of his body, writing: "An ash coffin made plain without any manner of superfluities, the corpse to be wrapped in cheap flannel, the expense of which I leave my wearing clothes to defray, as also the digging of the grave." His shoes were given to the gravedigger.

John Woolman is worth remembering because, more than most Christians, he kept his inner and outer life together. In the happy expression employed by Elizabeth O'Connor, this man of travel engaged, at the same time, in both an inward and an outward journey.[15] The inward journey was marked by an unusual sense of holy obedience. "I have been more and more instructed," he wrote near the end, "as to the necessity of depending, . . . upon the fresh instructions of Christ, the prince of peace, from day to day." The outward journey was marked by an increasing sensitivity to suffering and to an intelligent effort to eliminate as much of this suffering as is humanly possible.

What is most remarkable in Woolman's potent example is the complete bridging of the chasm that so mars our current Christian scene. His devotional experience and his social concern, far from being in conflict, actually required each other. He was acutely conscious of the danger of a social witness that could have become hard and cruel in its denunciation of others. "Christ knoweth," he said, "when the fruit-bearing branches themselves have need of purging." Being highly conscious of the way in which he shared the dangers of other finite men,

15 Elizabeth O'Connor, *Journey Inward, Journey Outward* (New York: Harper & Row, 1968).

he added, "Oh! that these lessons may be remembered by me!"[16]

Though John Woolman is generally recognized as the one who has best exemplified the Quaker ideal, there is a deep sense in which he is among the least sectarian, as he is among the least provincial of men. His non-Quaker readers far exceed those of his own group, and he can speak to puzzled men and women of the twentieth century quite as he appealed to those of his own. As in all examples of greatness, he transcended both the local and the temporal scenes. There is nothing sectarian or dated about one who is a really good person, whatever his denomination and whatever his age, because deep calls to deep. The paradox of Woolman is part of the general paradox of the terrible meek. Because he combined "holy boldness" with a sensitive tenderness, because he hated oppression and yet loved the oppressor, he belongs to all men who are seeking to be faithful in their own particular generations. It tells us something important about the human spirit to know that the writings and character of one of the most modest of men are still valid objects of attention after the passage of two hundred years.

The remarkable fact about the man of Mt. Holly was that, to a degree seldom matched, he was a whole man. He combined, in a really exciting fashion, a life of prayer, an acute social consciousness, and an unusually clear mentality. This is why it is valuable to recover his memory as vividly as possible. We do not know of anyone living in the last third of the twentieth century who can provide a pattern for our time as clearly as can a man who died shortly before the Declaration of Independence. Wholeness is so rare that it is universally valuable.

[16] *Journal, op. cit.*, pp. 314, 315.

Though we may fail to achieve the threefold standard, our own lives are made better by our knowing what the standard is. We may not achieve it, but at least we know when we fail.

It is good for us to encounter a person of the character of John Woolman, not for the purpose of glorifying either a man or an age, but to enable us to find a pattern adaptable to our own generation. The technology of the eighteenth century differed from that of our own century, but the human problems were essentially the same, and the fundamental solutions of those problems were the same. Much of the agony of our racial problem is a further confirmation of the truth that there is a moral law, and that failure to follow it brings consequences for a very long time. Slavery was a sin, the consequences of which cannot be stopped. Since we are in an unavoidable predicament in this regard, we need all of the help that we can get in order to learn how to handle it. One important form of assistance is that of learning how sensitive persons have tried earlier to live both compassionately and intelligently.

We live in a time of greatness. There is evidence of greatness even in our recognition of the enormity and complexity of our human problems. "The greatness of man is great," said Blaise Pascal over three hundred years ago, "in that he knows himself to be miserable."[17] But this is by no means the end of the story. No one in his senses can doubt the greatness of the achievement of the Apollo flights. Possibly the most encouraging feature of the first moon landing, more carefully observed than any other event in all previous history, has been the way in which it has led to reverence. There seemed, on that day, to be a complete absence of conceit as the most

[17] *Pensées*, 397.

sophisticated observers expressed their reverence unabashedly. This is a good sign. At his best moments, man is reverent, as well as compassionate and intelligent. That the vision of wholeness is still appealing is, in every way, a sign of hope and an indication of what is possible in the future. An important ministry, therefore, is the ministry of encouragement to those who are dissatisfied with the division that they observe, though they may be doubtful about the way to turn.

III

The Cultivation of Reverence

My business is with myself.
SAMUEL JOHNSON

WE SHALL never have a better world until there are better persons in it. No amount of economic or social planning, however important that may be, will ever succeed unless the plans are implemented by people with the right spirit. Every production of any value begins within, though it does not end there. The best social system we can imagine is bound to fail unless

59

the persons who participate in it are not only compassionate, but also self-disciplined and truly humble. In the words of William Penn, we must be changed men ourselves before we set out to change others. And we cannot be changed in the right direction without the cultivation of reverence.

The new man for our time, the truly contemporary man who is the whole man, will be concerned about the overcoming of war, poverty, and racial discrimination, but if he permits these to be his only objects of concern, they will become more elusive than they now are. Only by a conscious and continuing nurture of his inner life can any man avoid the tragedy of killing the thing he loves. The man who supposes that he has no time to pray or to reflect, because the social tasks are numerous and urgent, will soon find that he has become fundamentally unproductive, because he will have separated his life from its roots. It will not then be surprising if, in his promotion of what seems to him to be a good cause, he becomes bitter in his condemnation of others. Without the concurrent cultivation of the inner and the outer life, it is almost inevitable that a man deeply involved in social action should become self-righteous.

The specific problems of poverty and universal education involve a few elements of novelty, but the problems of the inner lives of those who work on poverty and education are not new at all. So far as can be discerned, there are no new sins; and it is doubtful that there is any new wisdom reserved for our time. In the cultivation of the inner life the dangers are always legion. There may be, in any specific situation, only one way of doing what is right, but there are always numerous ways of doing what is wrong. It is good, in this connection, to remember Chesterton's pertinent observation:

"It is always simple to fall; there are an infinity of angles at which one falls, only one at which one stands."[1] Though truth, as Aristotle recognized, is of the nature of the finite, error is of the nature of the infinite. We are fortunate in the fact that there has been a sifting process through the centuries. In the long dialogue participated in by the thoughtful people who have meditated seriously upon the problems of the life of devotion, many heresies have been so well exposed that contemporary men and women need not be seduced by them. It is helpful to know that several modern fads are simply ancient heresies in slight disguise.

Because we cannot reasonably expect to erect a constantly expanding structure of social activism upon a constantly diminishing foundation of faith, attention to the cultivation of the inner life is our first order of business, even in a period of rapid social change. The Church, if it is to affect the world, must become a center from which new spiritual power emanates. While the Church must be secular in the sense that it operates in the world, if it is only secular it will not have the desired effect upon the secular order which it is called upon to penetrate. With no diminution of concern for people, we can and must give new attention to the production of a trustworthy religious experience. In this understanding the devotional classics constitute a valuable resource.

One of the most remarkable features of the genuine classics of the inner life is their mutual corroboration. The religious experience of one man in one century may be suspected of having only subjective reference, but when the experiences are repeated in widely different cultures and epochs, we begin

---

[1] *Orthodoxy* (New York: John Lane Co., 1909), p. 186.

to have the only evidence of objectivity that men are ever able to achieve. Just as agreement in experience is the only reason for asserting objectivity in science, so it is the only reason for asserting it in religion. In the effort to know what is true, the most important fellowship is the fellowship of verification, in which the experience of one man supports the credibility of the experience of another. In the words of William James, "There is a certain composite photograph of saintliness."[2] Dean Inge gave expression to the entire logical structure of the experiential argument. "On all questions about religion," he said, "there is the most distressing divergency. But the saints do not contradict one another. They claim to have had glimpses of a land that is very far off, and they prove that they have been there by bringing back perfectly consistent and harmonious reports of it." Furthermore, said Inge, "We need not trouble ourselves to ask, and we could seldom guess without asking, whether a paragraph describing the highest spiritual experiences was written in the Middle Ages or in modern times, in the north or south of Europe, by a Catholic or by a Protestant."[3]

One of the most evident weaknesses of the contemporary church appears here. Even in an otherwise strong local church, it is not uncommon to find that most of the members, while they have undertaken some study of the Bible, particularly in Sunday School, are totally ignorant of the great chain of devotional literature extending from Augustine to Thomas Kelly and beyond. What is most surprising, in this connection, is the failure on the part of pastors to introduce those under their

[2] *The Varieties of Religious Experience* (New York: Longmans, Green and Company, 1903), p. 271.
[3] *Studies of English Mystics* (New York: Dutton, 1906), p. 35.

care to the acknowledged masters of the inner life. Though we might reasonably expect that almost every pastor would conduct classes pointed in this direction, only a tiny minority actually do so. The average pastor is a dedicated man eager to build up the spiritual life of the members and, through them, to affect the events of the world, but he normally omits one of the best ways of achieving this purpose. Pastors prepare sermons and visit families, but many seem to forget that in the New Testament the work of a pastor is linked to that of a teacher (Eph. 4:11). There is normally no lack of emphasis upon social issues, and this is good, but the odd outcome is that pastors seem to teach least in the very area in which they might be expected to have the greatest competence.

Because of the remarkable unanimity of judgment, the problem of selection among the classics is not a serious one. We have a manageable number of books on the cultivation of the interior life which have met the test of changing times and are therefore not on trial. Among these are the following:

The Confessions of St. Augustine.

The Imitation of Christ by Thomas à Kempis and others.

The Private Devotions of Lancelot Andrewes.

The Devotions of John Donne.

The Pensées of Blaise Pascal.

The Journal of John Woolman.

A Serious Call to a Devout and Holy Life by William Law.

A Testament of Devotion by Thomas Kelly.

These eight books are by no means all that serious seekers ought to study, but they are sufficient, when perused consecutively and prayerfully, to make a difference in almost any individual life. Though they can be studied profitably by lone individuals, they make more impact when studied with a group, because each student contributes to the others and thereby the experience is made richer.

It is a serious mistake to suppose that the only authors who are helpful in the development of a deeper religious experience are those normally classified as religious writers. As a matter of fact, some of the most helpful are those who are known almost solely as secular authors. An excellent example of such a group is Dr. Samuel Johnson (1709-1784). Part of the strength of such a guide, so far as modern man is concerned, resides precisely in the fact that, though he was thoroughly and unashamedly devout, Johnson was not professionally religious. The famous lexicographer was rough or even uncouth in his manners, and he was completely intolerant of cant or pretense, but his example of personal piety is all the more valuable in consequence. He helps us partly because he had, himself, been helped by other giants, chiefly Jeremy Taylor and William Law. He liked to remember, he said, the precept of Taylor, "Never lie in your prayers; never confess more than you really believe; never promise more than you mean to perform." William Law was, Johnson said, "more than a match" for him.

For those who are denied access to complete books, there is the possibility of concentrating upon selections. Further depth of understanding may come from the reading of the books of contemporary authors who have made it their task to interpret the works of the classic devotional writers. Among these, one of the most helpful is Rufus M. Jones, who, at the height of his powers, wrote books with such titles as *Spiritual Energies in Daily Life, The World Within*, and *The Testimony of the Soul*. In this last-mentioned volume, Dr. Jones, as early as 1936, undertook to write a chapter on the very topic that is concerning so many of us in the contemporary scene, "The Inner Life and the Social Order." Douglas V. Steere, Rufus Jones' immediate successor in the philosophy chair at Haverford College, has likewise contributed volumes of interpretation and analysis, introducing many readers to rich veins of which they would otherwise have been largely ignorant. Characteristic titles of Dr. Steere are *On Beginning from Within* and *Doors into Life*. The latter volume introduces the reader to five classics, *The Imitation of Christ*, *Introduction to the Devout Life* by Francis de Sales, John Woolman's *Journal*, Søren Kierkegaard's *Purity of Heart*, and the *Selected Letters* of Friedrich von Hügel.

Another important contemporary interpreter of classic spiritual experience is John Baillie, particularly in *The Diary of Private Prayer* and *Christian Devotion*, the latter published posthumously by the efforts of his widow. In the United States one of the best of living interpreters is Howard Thurman, author of *The Inward Journey* and *Disciplines of the Spirit*. Dr. Thurman has profited greatly by his careful study of the Negro spirituals. An interpreter who is sorely missed is the late Thomas Kepler of Oberlin who, in spite of severe physical stress near the end of his life, found strength to bring out reprints of the books mentioned for the use of the general public.

Nearly all of the classics of devotion have in common the conviction of the possibility and, indeed, actuality of the divine-human encounter. Impressed as the spiritual giants may be with the natural order, they are seldom willing to settle for this as the only or the sufficient revelation of the Divine Mind. Though most would agree with Wordsworth in his sense of reverence in the midst of natural beauty, they do not stop there. William Temple was representing faithfully the major tradition when, after speaking of God's revelation as an indirect one through the natural order, he went on to affirm the possibility and actuality of direct communication between God and the finite human soul. "It would be strange," Temple wrote, "if He acted only in the inorganic and non-spiritual, and dealt with spirits akin to Himself only by the indirect testimony of the rest of His creation."[4]

It is a mark of serious decline in theology that many contemporary students have never read a line from the great books of William Temple and that some students do not even know or recognize his name. We get some idea of how quickly fashions change when we remember that Temple's major work was completed as late as 1934. Partly because he had deep respect for scientific method, Temple's whole philosophy was radically empirical. Consequently, he found it necessary to pay serious attention to the reports of spiritual experience. Because he noted that the standard experience reported by the saints was a personal one, Temple was forced, in intellectual honesty, to think of God as a Person.

We often hear the criticism that the Church is afflicted with piety, but the real trouble is that its piety is not deep enough! Since the materials are available, all that is needed is the recognition of where they are, and the will to employ them. An important contribution would be the liberation of the term "piety" from its present damaging connotations, reinstating it as a term of respect. We, indeed, still have a little piety; we say a few hasty prayers; we sing meaningfully a few hymns; we read snatches from the Bible. But all of this is far removed from the massive dose that we sorely need if we are to be the men and women who can perform a healing service in our generation. The seat of our disease, says Helmut Thielicke, "is not in the branches of our nerves at all but rather in our

[4] *Nature, Man and God* (London: Macmillan and Co., 1934), p. 318.

roots which are stunted and starved."[5] The eloquent German points out that Martin Luther prayed four hours each day, "not despite his busy life but because only so could he accomplish his gigantic labors." Luther worked so hard that a little desultory praying would not suffice. "To work without praying and without listening," continues Thielicke, "means only to grow and spread oneself upward, without striking roots and without an equivalent in the earth."[6] Trees can grow well in rocky soil, as I can attest by looking out the window of my mountain writing cabin, but they do this only by finding crevices in the rocks where the roots are able to penetrate deeply.

The more we consider the appropriateness of the organic metaphor, the more we are impressed with the explosive power of a seed. It is no accident that among the best known and best loved of all the parables of Christ are those of the seeds and the soils (Mark 4:1-32). The idea of the effectiveness of leaven, an idea that seems common and unexciting to us because we have heard it often, was once original. The word "leaven" does not appear in the Old Testament in a figurative sense, though it appears many times in a literal sense. The fact that leaven becomes figurative in the teaching of Christ is one of the most important aspects of that teaching. Prior to Christ's time, the prophets of Israel had made use of the concept of "remnant," which, though it has some superficial resemblance to leaven, is really very different. The remnant, which can be kept pure and undefiled in spite of the surrounding corruption of the world, is fundamentally a defensive idea, while leaven is profoundly aggressive. Leaven penetrates the dough

[5] *The Waiting Father* (New York: Harper & Row, 1959), p. 65.
[6] *Ibid.*, pp. 65, 66.

as salt penetrates the meat; it can never perform its function so long as it exists in splendid isolation.

The wonderful thing about seed is that it wants to get out. Near where this is being written is a toadstool that, in the night, broke through the asphalt surface of our parking lot, lifting into the air a disk of asphalt nearly three inches in diameter. This provides some hint of how the supposed conflict between pietism and activism is overcome. If the deep underground vitality is adequately nourished, i.e., if the life of devotion is genuine, it will be bound to crack the economic and political barriers. In fact, it cannot be stopped in its redemptive process. Like the mustard seed, it will produce "large branches, so that the birds of the air can make nests in its shade" (Mark 4:32). This is how the Kingdom grows. First a few people are deeply changed, then they sink their spiritual roots into the soil of God's love, and then the conditions under which they and their brothers live are changed. Renewal begins on the inside.

When we begin to ask what the conditions of inner renewal are, we receive essentially the same answers from nearly all of those whom we have most reason to respect. One major answer is the emphasis upon discipline. In the conduct of one's own life it is soon obvious, as many have learned the hard way, that empty freedom is a snare and a delusion. In following what comes naturally or easily, life simply ends in confusion, and in consequent disaster. Without the discipline of time, we spoil the next day the night before, and without the discipline of prayer, we are likely to end by having practically no experience of the divine-human encounter. However compassionate we may be with others, we dare not be soft or indulgent with ourselves. Excellence comes at a price, and one of the major prices is that of inner control.

We have not advanced very far in our spiritual lives if we have not encountered the basic paradox of freedom, to the effect that we are most free when we are bound. But not just any way of being bound will suffice; what matters is the character of our binding. The one who would like to be an athlete, but who is unwilling to discipline his body by regular exercise and by abstinence, is not free to excel on the field or the track. His failure to train rigorously and to live abstemiously denies him the freedom to go over the bar at the desired height, or to run with the desired speed and endurance. With one concerted voice the giants of the devotional life apply the same principle to the whole of life with the dictum: *Discipline is the price of freedom.*

The same principle applies to the arts, particularly music. The people who sit comfortably, listening to a trained orchestra, can have only a fragmentary appreciation of the price that the musicians on the platform have already paid. Many of these musicians have learned that they must practice every day, regardless of how they feel or of what the interruption may be. Even the least acceptance of laxity may lead to mediocrity or worse. Many force themselves to practice scales, realizing that the precise senses of touch and hearing will deteriorate apart from steady use.

Those without direct experience in counseling new authors can hardly believe how many people there are who wish that they could be writers, and could have their literary works published.[7] In an astonishing number of cases, however, these are fair-weather writers. They write a few pages when the inspiration is strong, but they cannot endure the experience of

[7] In the Workshops for Christian Writers, organized by Charlie Shedd and supported in part, by the Lilly Endowment, the applications far exceed the number of those who can be accepted.

fastening themselves to a writing desk morning after morning. A great many books, and possibly too many books, are published each year, but the unpublished manuscripts far outnumber the published ones. The unfinished manuscripts are legion because it is so much easier to start than to follow through to the bitter end. It is doubtful if any work of excellence is ever produced without some discouragement and without days when the producer goes on doggedly, not because he likes it, but because he knows that this is the only way in which any work of importance is ever completed.

It is part of our good fortune that some of the noblest of authors have told us how they have operated. Thus Dr. Samuel Johnson has explained how he finished writing his demanding work, *The Lives of the Poets*, which he at last completed in March, 1781, when he was seventy-one years of age. He wrote it, he says, in his usual way "unwilling to work, and working with vigour and haste." What is often unknown is that the sage of London, who produced so much literature against his natural will, applied the same wisdom about life to the knowledge of God, with the result that his piety was, in Boswell's words, "constant and fervent." One consequence of this interior discipline is the existence of a hundred written prayers, many of them composed at the major turning points of Johnson's career, such as that of starting to compose the Dictionary of the English Language. On this august occasion, which, in spite of his prodigious learning, was frightening even to Johnson, he wrote:

O God who hast hitherto supported me, enable me to proceed in this labour, and in the whole task of my present state; that when I shall render up, at the last day, an account of the talent committed to me, I may receive pardon, for the sake of Jesus Christ. Amen.[8]

Johnson may be rightly regarded as one of the giants of the inner life who have understood very well the necessity of regularity in devotional experience. He attended public worship, often against his temporary inclination, because he understood that he needed constant reminding. Recognizing his failures when alone, he set great store by public worship, not because he felt spiritually strong, but because he recognized that he was weak. Knowing, by repeated experience, how fruitless empty freedom can be, he put much thought into the establishment of a rule of life. One good example of his recognition of the need of a rule to live by is his Diary entry for Easter Eve, the 18th of April, 1772, a time of year when he normally reviewed and sought to renew his spiritual vitality. Part of his jottings for that day are as follows:

I hope to cast my time into some stated method.
To let no hour pass unemployed.
To rise by degrees more early in the morning.
To keep a Journal.
I hope to read the whole Bible once a year as long as I live.[9]

It was Johnson's general practice at this period of his life to read the New Testament in Greek, though he employed an English translation for the Old Testament. His repeated personal discipline included the discipline of prayer, the discipline of worship, the discipline of time, and the discipline of charity. Though his business, as he said unforgettably, was

[8] Most of the handwritten prayers of Dr. Johnson are deposited in the library of Pembroke, his old college at Oxford. In 1945 they were published by Harper & Brothers, but the volume is now out of print.
[9] *Diaries Prayers and Annals* (New Haven: Yale University Press, 1958), p. 147.

with himself, he understood that an important part of his own life was his responsibility to others.

Johnson's personal honesty was as striking as was his determination to bring order into his troubled life, and part of his honesty lay in his frank recognition that his rule had not been wholly kept. He was especially conscious of such failure in the spring of 1781 when there occurred the death of his friend and benefactor, Henry Thrale. Easter was that year, for him, an unusually reverent occasion, and part of his religious exercise was his admission of partial failure:

> I hope that since my last Communion I have advanced by pious reflections in my submission to God, and my benevolence to Man, but I have corrected no external habits, nor have kept any of the resolutions made in the beginning of the year, yet I hope still to be reformed, and not to lose my whole life in idle purposes. Many years are already gone, irrevocably past in useless Misery; that what remains may be spent better, grant O God.[10]

While we easily realize the need of careful effort and instruction in the acquirement of minor skills, we often fail to see this when it comes to the noblest of all human enterprises. If it is a bold venture to try to come into meaningful confrontation with another finite mind, it is a far bolder venture to try to encounter the Divine Mind. We have two apparently inseparable barriers, not found in ordinary human understanding: the dissimilarity and inequality of the partners in the encounter, and the complete freedom from bodily limitation on the divine side of the mutual communication. If spiritual intercourse with another finite individual is an amazing leap across a chasm, which separates the personalities even of those who love each other dearly, intercourse with the Infinite

[10] *Ibid.*, p. 305.

Person is more amazing, because the chasm that separates is incalculably greater. A man who prays is engaging in the most ambitious of all undertakings and therefore he needs all of the help that he can get. That is why, if we are wise, we shall pay very careful attention to Christ's personal example of prayer.

Among the important lessons that the spiritual giants can teach us, and on which they have striking agreement, is that we are not likely to experience reality in prayer unless we practice a great deal of silent waiting. Far from prayer being a matter of words, it is often, at its best, freedom from words, since our own chatter can prevent our listening. Important as it may be for us to express our deepest desires to God, much as a little child expresses his desires to his earthly father, it is even more important to be truly receptive in order to learn what the Divine Father is trying to say to us. This is because, though we already know what we want, we do not know what God wants.

One of the finest of interior disciplines, practiced by those whom we have most reason to admire, is that of a period of deliberate receptivity at or near the beginning of the conscious day. Some who have gone deeply into the life of the spirit, report that they begin the day by saying "Lord, I am ready to listen. Speak to me now." Then the individual is quiet, not in the sense of being merely inactive or dull, but in the sense of being vibrantly attentive. The results of this discipline are much more productive than the world normally knows. After all, it is an intelligent practice to get one's marching orders before one moves, for movement may be in the wrong direction. No one claims to hear an audible voice, such as could be reproduced on a tape recorder; what is reported is something far more profound, i.e., a sense of direct leading. Because this sense of leading is not always clear, the devout person never claims infallibility in reception. What is given, by the modest practice of listening, is often a new direction, and the new road is frequently better than the one that would have been traveled otherwise.

An impressive example of the value of the discipline of starting the day with a period of listening for God's guidance, and of asking instructions for the day, is that provided by the Iona Community of Scotland. This is the major discipline that holds all members of the Iona Fellowship together, wherever they may be. To a remarkable degree, their practice meets the test of social verification, since the way in which this small minority of disciplined men have penetrated the economic, educational, and religious life of their country is striking indeed. They are changing society because they have *been* changed.

Powerful and productive as individual silence may be, group silence may be even more productive. Many are able to report that a genuine entering into a group silence, when it is dynamic and not merely sleepy, can bring, in the briefest conceivable time, an entire flood of ideas not previously recognized. More than three hundred years ago, Robert Barclay, one of the acknowledged masters of the interior life, had such an experience that radically altered his succeeding career. "When I came into the silent assemblies of God's people," he reported, "I felt a secret power among them, which touched my heart, and as I gave way unto it, I found the evil weakening in me, and the good raised up, and so I became thus knit and united unto them, hungering more and more after the increase of this power and life, whereby I might feel myself perfectly redeemed."[11] That the experience did not end with spiritual elation is demonstrated by the degree to which the Scottish thinker succeeded in helping to stop religious persecution and to assist colonization in America.

The experience with group silence reported by Howard Thurman, who has already been mentioned, is not dissimilar to that of Barclay. The fact that one of these experiences came in the seventeenth century and the other in the twentieth century is insignificant, since the two men share in the fellowship of verification. Dr. Thurman's report includes the paradox of powerful movement arising out of shared stillness:

> After some time, I am not sure precisely when, the sense of the movement of my spirit disappeared and a great living stillness engulfed me. And then a strange thing happened. There came into my mind, as if on a screen, first a single word and then more words, until there was in my mind's eye an entire sentence from the Sermon on the Mount. The curious thing was that, familiar as I was with the passage, one part of my mind waited for each word to appear as the sentence built, while another part knew what the sentence was going to say. When it was all there, with avidity my mind seized upon it. I began thinking about it as the text of what I would say. When I was ready to speak, I placed my hands on the railing in front of me and was about to stand, when from behind me came the voice of a lady quoting that passage.[12]

Silence, as Dr. Thurman and many others have realized, is of different kinds. Physical silence, while normally a prerequisite, is never sufficient. "Once the physical silencing has been achieved," says Dr. Thurman, "then the real work must

---

11 *Apology*, XI, vii.
12 *Disciplines of the Spirit* (New York: Harper & Row, 1963), p. 97. The scene of the incident was the Coulter Street Meetinghouse, Germantown, Philadelphia.

begin."[13] The increasing difficulty of finding silence in the modern world is one price we pay for our supposedly sophisticated age. Most of our vaunted gadgets are sound-enhancing rather than sound-diminishing. The only reasonable conclusion is that people do not really desire silence.

Through many centuries of Christian experience, men and women of all stations and of different nations have learned that the most potent means of growth in the life of the spirit is contemplation of the life and teachings of Jesus Christ. Some have followed and recommended the practice of reading short sections of the Gospels every day of their lives, no matter how busy they may be, and no matter where they are. In regular confrontation with Christ they meet One who is like themselves in that He could suffer, as He could be tempted, yet who is superior to them in that they have reason to believe Him when He says that He truly reveals the Father. As men center their lives upon Him, they encounter something even better than silence, and may finally come to the conclusion that the God of all the world is actually like Jesus Christ. This is the most exciting idea that can enter the human mind, for, if God is really like Christ, then the things that matter most are not at the mercy of the things that matter least, and the greatest thing in the world is caring (I Cor. 13:13).

At the heart of religious experience, if it is genuine, there is neither "a primitive absurdity nor a sophisticated truism," but "a momentous possibility."[14] The more deeply an honest man concentrates his attention upon Christ, the more he comes to the conclusion that the momentous possibility is an actuality.

[13] *Ibid.*, p. 98.
[14] W. P. Montague, *Belief Unbound* (New Haven: Yale University Press, 1930), p. 6.

One of the first results of meditation on Christ's life and teaching is the revelation that ensues concerning ourselves. "Meditate on His life," wrote à Kempis, "and thou wilt be ashamed to find how far removed thou art from His perfection."[15] Direct confrontation with Christ gives what is required for the deepest devotional experience, because such confrontation reveals to us both our own unworthiness and our basic hope, both our separation from God and our potential reconciliation with Him. It is almost impossible to confront Christ without consequent prayer, and the experience is not likely to be long continued without amendment of life.

Once we have accepted the necessity of voluntary discipline, have learned to value silence, and have concentrated our attention upon Christ, we have not completed the inward journey, but we are well on the road. There is not then and there never will be complete freedom from problems, but there is at least a firm stance in which problems may be met as they arise. The school of prayer is one from which no person is ever graduated.

No man can do enough for others if he is always surrounded by others. Every follower of Christ is bound to be impressed by His well-known words about solitary prayer, "Go into your room and shut the door and pray to your Father who is in secret" (Matt. 6:6). Part of the significance of these words lies not only in the avoidance of the distraction that other people create, but, even more, in the elimination of the temptation to make the spiritual life a matter of display or ostentation. The great value of being alone in our deepest experience is that solitariness transcends the tendency to try to impress.

[15] *Imitation*, Book I, Chapter 25.

Sometimes we need freedom from such a tendency, avoiding even the companionship of those whom we most love and trust. It is difficult in the modern crowded world to go apart, as Jesus repeatedly did, but we must nevertheless try to add this resource to our hectic lives. The Kirkridge Fellowship of Bangor, Pennsylvania, a fellowship based upon, and in some ways similar to, that of Iona, shows great wisdom in encouraging each of its members to arrange a six-hour solitary retreat each month. Those who are able to manage this have experienced a remarkable inner strength.

If there is a time when we grow alone, there is also a time when we grow with others. The claim that we ought never to pray with others because Christ said to pray alone is clearly fallacious. To show that Christ wept does not deny that He also laughed, and to say that He advocated solitary devotion is not to deny that He recognized the value of group devotion. That He actually appreciated the value of such devotion is shown by His own recorded experience, especially that on the Mount of Transfiguration (Mark 9:2-8), and also by his explicit statement that where His followers were together, there He was (Matt. 18:20).

No man is strong enough or devout enough to operate alone. Even solitary worship is much more productive if it is enriched by the remembered experience of gathered worship. Iron sharpens iron (Prov. 27:17). It is literally true, in the best experiences of joint worship, that the whole is greater than the sum of the parts. Though there may be religions in which solitariness is the highest expression of devotion, this is never true for the Christian, who understands that, bad as the Church may be, life without it is worse. The point is not that men *cannot* worship alone, but rather that they are more likely to be invigorated and sent out into the world as new persons if they are participants in the joint experience of a loving and reverent company of their fellow seekers.

The emphasis upon inner development, when fully considered, turns out to be the most unselfish of enterprises, because, as we live for one another, the best we can give is ourselves. A man has made a step toward a genuine maturity when he realizes that, though he ought to perform kind and just acts, the greatest gift he can provide others consists in being a radiant and encouraging person. What we are is more significant, in the long run, than what we do. It is impossible for a man to give what he does not have.

IV

The Life of Service

Nothing stamped with the Divine image and likeness
was sent into the world to be trodden on, and degraded,
and imbruted by its fellows.

ABRAHAM LINCOLN

IT IS POSSIBLE to be religious, in the sense of having the assurance of personal salvation, and yet be blind or insensitive to vast areas of human suffering. While it is true that life is never adequate without reverence, it is true, at the same time, that no experience is valid unless it leads to acts of justice and mercy. Grace can be appropriated too cheaply! The author

81

of the Fourth Gospel provided a balance to the Synoptics when, in his account of the Last Supper, he indicated that Christians are asked to combine the basin and the towel with the bread and the wine (John 13:3-17).

One of the insidious dangers of any religion is spiritualism. Spiritualism is demonstrated whenever people become satisfied with what goes on in a place of worship with no real worry about the poverty adjacent to it. It was part of the immense contribution of Archbishop William Temple that he pointed out, nearly forty years ago, the danger inherent in all spiritual religion affirming that the Christian faith, when it understands itself, never settles for this heresy. "Christianity," he wrote in a frequently quoted sentence, "is the most avowedly materialist of all the great religions."[1] What he meant was that the Christian faith is never satisfied with inner states, including even the blissful contemplation of the divine, but is always concerned with bodies. It is the concern with bodies, as well as with spirits, that has led to the founding of hospitals and to programs of child feeding. Such enterprises, thought Temple, are not peripheral, but central, because the major conviction is that the Word became *flesh* (John 1:14). The word "flesh" was chosen, it would seem, because of its frankly materialistic association. The follower of Christ does not ignore or deny the material order, but asserts its reality and undertakes its subordination.

There cannot be a total gospel unless it includes the social gospel. This is not because human beings are uniformly good or even deserving, but because God's care includes both the undeserving and the deserving, as it includes both spirits and

---

[1] *Nature, Man and God, op. cit.,* p. 478.

bodies. Some form of social gospel is required if each man is recognized as being the object of God's care, and if, consequently, each is his brother's brother. I cannot be wholly saved unless my brother is saved because, in the unforgettable words of John Donne, "I am involved in mankind."[2]

Once we are really clear about the idea that Christianity, while it is spiritual, must always be *more* than spiritual, we become aware of the current dangers of which, otherwise, we might easily be too tolerant. One of the most important of these dangers has to do with drugs. Many of those who defend the use of LSD claim that its users constitute a religion, and in this claim they are, in one sense, correct. There is no doubt that LSD users report mystical experiences, including a vivid sense of elation and freedom from the limitations of ordinary mundane existence. When controlled experiments have been made, with theological students participating, the mystical experiences reported by those who have taken the drug are sometimes more vivid than are those of the nonusers. If the only element in religion is personal ecstasy, the drug religion meets the test.

The fallacy inherent in the religious claims of those who take drugs for the purpose of "mind expansion" lies not in what they include, but in what they omit. Even though some drug mystics also have some social concerns, there is no evidence of a causal relationship between the ecstasy and the concern. It is preposterous to suppose that a pot orgy leads to the kind of sensitivity about human suffering that is represented in the classic example of John Woolman. Seekers of ecstasy are being religious, even when they are not theistic,

---

[2] *Devotions upon Emergent Occasions* (Ann Arbor Paperbacks, The University of Michigan Press, 1959), p. 109.

but any religion that seeks to produce inner feelings, and no more, is addressing itself to only a fragment of what is needed for the abundant life.

Whether drug cultists should be accorded the legal and other privileges that are now granted religious societies hinges largely on a matter of definition, but that is not a very important consideration. What is important is that thoughtful people should not be taken in by cults that deny the criterion of wholeness. We must be sufficiently tough-minded to examine long-time results and not temporary elation only. What happens when the hallucination fades? Does it aid in the development of more courage, as well as more compassion? These are the hard questions that those who are satisfied with a sentimental tolerance will not bother to ask.

The drug religion is really a new form of pietism, and it belongs to the pietist camp precisely because it involves no social gospel. It stresses rapture, but rapture is very far from being the major or sole aspect of a healthy religion. Though in one sense this particular form of pietism is new, in another sense it is not, for the emphasis on rapture alone is a very old heresy. Men simply have different ways of producing it in different ages. The late Edith Hamilton helped us to realize that the essential weakness of the mystery religions of ancient Greece appeared at precisely this point. Because the mysteries produced ecstasy, but nothing more, they had no power to alter the moral structure of society.

The practice of speaking with tongues, in spite of many differences, belongs to the same pietist classification. Glossolalia, the gift of tongues, which was well known in New Testament times and in many subsequent periods, has had a strong revival in our generation, not only among Pentecostal

sects, but also among otherwise conventional Christian denominations. The essence of the experience is that people under
strong emotional excitement begin to use syllables that are not
easily understood, even by themselves. Some have asserted that
such speaking is the one and only external evidence of the
gift of the Holy Spirit.

Though speaking with tongues undoubtedly occurs, and
though it usually does no harm, the practice is very far from
the center of the Christian spectrum. It is off center because it
has no redemptive social consequences. There is no evidence
that it leads men and women who engage in the practice to
become more dedicated in feeding the hungry or in changing
repressive laws. It is religious, we have to admit, but it is lacking in ethical content. Though we ought not to discourage
anyone from speaking with tongues because, personally, it
may be a lifting experience, it is nevertheless our duty to show
how far removed it is from a total gospel, which includes both
the experiential and the ethical aspects of the one faith. The
ultimate assessment of this particular form of pietism was made
by the Apostle Paul when he asserted that even if he were to
speak with the tongues of men and of angels, but had no love,
the outcome was inadequate (I Cor. 13:1). We must remember
that the famous sentence, just paraphrased, was directed to the
members of a local church in which speaking with tongues was
highly regarded. Paul's major point was that the tongue-speaker
is indulging in what is essentially self-centered, rather than
brother-centered. "He who speaks in a tongue edifies himself,
but he who prophesies edifies the church" (I Cor. 14:4). Paul
upheld the practice of glossolalia but, at the same time, he also
pointed out its limitations, which are those of any religious
experience devoid of either logical or social content. "I would

rather," he wrote, "speak five words with my mind, in order to instruct others, than ten thousand words in a tongue" (I Cor. 14:19). This conclusion, which demonstrates the essential tough-mindedness of the Apostle to the Gentiles, requires very little more in either explanation or emendation.

Once we are convinced that inner religion, necessary as it is, will never suffice, we are in a position to ask ourselves how the social witness of the followers of Christ can be rightly made. We know that social sins, as well as individual sins, must be opposed, and that positive efforts must be made to establish a truly loving form of justice. It is obvious that mere goodwill is not enough. The Christian knows that love, in the sense of genuine caring, provides him with his major premise, but he is also aware that the minor premise must be supplied by hard thinking based upon experience. At what point does welfare payment cease to be beneficent and become harmful? Does the gift of more food really help if it is not accompanied by a program designed to avoid population increase? Since there are no easy answers to such questions, we are called to be wise as serpents while we are innocent as doves (Matt. 10:16).

The chief way in which the Church affects the surrounding social order is through its members. If the Church, by its group experience, in which the participants are given both new strength and new insight, sends people out to serve wherever their daily work places them, it is being really effective. Sometimes it is said, in harsh criticism, that a particular congregation has not done anything about the race question, but when we probe more deeply, we find that what is meant is only that the Church has not made a public statement. Perhaps the Church, in the person of its members, has done much to overcome racial bitterness. What if one of the members is a judge,

and, because of his Christian experience, he has made an unusual effort to see that equal justice is provided in the court?
What if a member is a merchant, and he has gone to great
lengths to provide equal opportunity in employment, not only
at the lower levels of work, but also in managerial capacities?
The truth is that this is now going on and it is going on in the
membership of congregations in which no official statements
have been made. We can be thankful for the witness of the
deed, as well as the witness of the word.

When critics complain that the Church does nothing, they
often betray a most naïve conception of what the Church is.
It cannot be pointed out too often, or insisted upon too
strongly, that *the Church is its members*. It is not a building,
as it is not an office in New York or in Geneva. It is *people*,
most of whom are operating in common life as homemakers,
engineers, ordinary workers, and professional men. It is these
who represent the Church, because it is these who *are* the
Church. In the long run, the effect that the Church has upon
the world will be made chiefly by people engaged in secular
occupations.

The best social order will come when a sufficient number
of people, located in positions that affect the structure of society, are motivated and trained to assist in producing the full-
est and freest life for others that is possible. The individual
Christian, unworthy as he may be, shares in Christ's central
purpose, which He expressed when He said, "I came that they
may have life, and have it abundantly" (John 10:10). Man is
too grand to waste, even though he is too miserable to save
himself.

We understand the idea of the Church better when we see
it as a functioning fellowship. What the merchant decides

while he prays and sings with other dedicated seekers, reaches its fulfillment on Monday morning when he hires new workers without prejudice and without sentimentality. It is the cumulative decisions of countless individuals by which the fate of nations and the character of an age are determined. Christopher Dawson is clarifying when he says that "what we are asserting is simply that individual acts of spiritual decision ultimately bear social fruit."[3] The Church is more than individuals, because it is the Body of Christ, but it would not even exist apart from the individuals who are the members of that Body.

When we have said that Christian social service is what ordinary Christians do in ordinary jobs, we have said something that is both true and important, but we dare not stop here. Sometimes corporate stands also need to be made. Though the initial impact of John Woolman's stand against slavery was made through the instrumentality of individuals who voluntarily liberated their fellow humans, this was not the entire story. It was also significant that Woolman's particular Christian fellowship took a united and public stand against slavery. It was essential to the social process that this public stand should not be taken prematurely or in such a manner as to produce bitterness on the part of the outvoted minority who were not convinced of the rightness of the step. This is the reason why Woolman held the manuscript of his first essay against slavery for eight years before he took the crucial step of publishing it.

Though the problem of public statements by Christian bodies is a difficult and complicated one, it is also one that cannot be avoided. The deepest difficulty is that of knowing

[3] *The Historic Reality of Christian Culture* (New York: Harper & Row, 1960), p. 18.

when the Church has actually spoken. When a statement is made about recognizing the government of Communist China or about unilateral withdrawal from South Vietnam, who is speaking? Is it the total Church? Is it a commission in a denominational headquarters, or what? One of the central issues involved in this problem is that of intellectual honesty. We are certainly dishonest if we make it appear that the entire Church is speaking when the voice is actually that of only a small group within the Church. Even a statement in a preface is insufficient to avoid confusion, because the news reports frequently neglect to include the qualifications of the original statement.[4] The issue is so pertinent that it has elicited a full-length treatment from a respected scholar.[5]

It is not necessary to conclude that the members of a church have to wait for complete unanimity before the corporate witness can be made, because, in many controversies, that would mean endless delay. What is needed is the kind of sensitivity that makes Christians know when there is sufficient agreement to make a statement truly representative of the main weight of Christian judgment. Admittedly, this is not easy, but it is something to be attempted. We succeed only in creating our own credibility gap when we act as though complex questions can have simple answers. Though in many political situations no one knows exactly what ought to be done, it can at least be seen that the simple answers are uniformly wrong.

Anyone who travels about the country, listening to his fel-

[4] An illustration of such confusion is that of a publication in England which the news media immediately called "The Quaker View of Sex," though it did not speak for all Quakers, and was promptly disavowed by official bodies.

[5] Paul Ramsey, *Who Speaks for the Church?* (Nashville: Abingdon Press, 1967).

low citizens, soon becomes aware of a widespread loss of respect for many of the most publicized undertakings of the social gospel. It is a serious mistake to dismiss this as a matter of ignorance, prejudice, or lack of social concern, since it is often expressed by those who are thoughtful and sensitive persons. Those of us who are involved in the struggles for social justice are foolish if we do not try to understand why much that we have done has backfired so unmistakably. What brings revulsion is not the aims of the crusaders, but the mood of moral arrogance that is often exhibited. What the average citizen finds disturbing is not the desire to overcome poverty or the desire to stop the war, but what one Christian leader has termed "profound, inexcusable spiritual egoism." One of the reasons why it is helpful to us now to sit humbly at the feet of John Woolman is that Woolman demonstrated the possibility of taking a courageous social stand without personal arrogance and without a sense of moral superiority to the persons whose acts were held to be unjust.

Fortunately, there are ways in which some of the respect that has been temporarily lost can be recovered. One way of recovering respect is the conscious and deliberate effort to encourage expressions of doubt. It is helpful, for example, for those who are deeply committed to the war against poverty to admit that in numerous sectors they do not know how to proceed and, furthermore, that some of the efforts undertaken with confidence have failed dismally. Moral crusaders can aid their own cause if they are willing to admit that, because they do not know all of the answers, they, too, belong to the fellowship of perplexity. Those who claim to know how to end the war in Vietnam might be listened to with respect if they were to admit that the only good solution is the least evil one.

Doubt need not mean weakness, but, in the long run, may actually become a source of strength. We shall accomplish much more if we begin by saying, "This may not be the right way to do it, but, because it is the best we can now see, we shall proceed."

It is good to be courageous on moral issues, but it is a serious mistake to suppose that courage requires a dogmatic certainty on the part of the protester. It is almost incredible, when we think of the complexities of modern society, that so many should feel so sure about what should be done. Part of the difficulty arises, no doubt, from the practice of carrying placards, because placards do not lend themselves to subtlety. One result of any slogan confrontation is that the issues are inevitably oversimplified. Since the placard has no room for a sophisticated statement, it often expresses nothing but a harsh imperative and easily descends to employment of abusive or even obscene language. This accounts, in large measure, for the backlash in the general public. After all, it is not surprising if ordinary people begin to lose respect for those who claim, on the one hand, to be actuated by a high moral purpose, yet who engage, on the other hand, in the use of epithets and personal abuse.

A second way in which respect for the social gospel can be regained is by the clear insistence, on the part of Christian leaders, that engagement in social struggles does not absolve a man of the requirements of personal morality. What many decent people find revolting, and what they ought to find revolting, is the widely held view that such matters as personal honesty, the payment of debts, and fidelity to marriage vows are no longer important because they have no bearing on social issues. Thus it is not unknown for a student who engages in the effort to increase voting registration in Mississippi, to pay no attention to the fact that he owes money in another state, and makes no gesture of payment to those who have trusted him. If this is the new morality, its novelty does not make it any more attractive to those who are hurt by it. It is never reasonable to believe in the moral integrity of any worker for justice if his concern does not involve not only compassion, but also common honesty and decency.

A third way in which the adherents of the social gospel can enhance their reputation and recover a greater degree of respect is by reaffirming a fundamentally religious approach to social issues. In the concerted effort to rehabilitate the word "secular," some Christian leaders have become more secular than anybody else, and have tried to make "secular" a new holy word. It is time to say clearly that the ultimate solution of our most difficult social problem, the problem of racial antagonism, will have to be a frankly religious one. Though economic and political approaches are important, they are never primary, even though they may provide both assistance and temporary relief. Laws we need, so that those who engage in repression, in connection with voting, housing, or employment, can be brought into court and dealt with as criminals, but laws do not change men's hearts.

A fourth way in which the general image of the social gospel can be improved is by the deliberate use of laughter, particularly at ourselves. One mistake that we have made in our Christian social witness is that we have been too uniformly serious. When we are disappointed with our fellow men and with ourselves, as we inevitably are, laughter is a solvent. It helps us greatly to know that Christ laughed, and to sense the variety of His humor. Some of His teachings, which are com-

pletely mystifying on the assumption that He was deadly serious, suddenly become clear if it is recognized that He was
joking. Part of the trouble with our standard protest marches
and sit-ins is not that they are lacking in moral emphasis, but
that they are, in one sense, too moral. Always there is some
claim about injustice or unfairness; always there is unqualified
condemnation of the opposition; always there is dead seriousness. We need to remember that it is possible to exhibit an
inverted Puritanism, and that the extreme concern for morals
is the essence of fanaticism. It is highly pertinent to our own
situation to know that some of the best of Christ's humor
refers to the predicament of the unlaughing Pharisee. The
claimant to self-righteousness is always a bit ridiculous, but he
could be saved from the worst excesses if he could stop and
laugh heartily. The recovery of laughter would be more than
a relief; it would be a genuine social service.

The race question, so far as the American social experiment
is concerned, began when the first slave was brought to the
western shores of the Atlantic Ocean and sold to some white
planter. That this white planter was possibly a Christian is
hard for us to understand, but we shall be less harsh in our
judgment when we realize that in another three hundred fifty
years, some of our actions may seem as incomprehensible to
our descendants as do those of our ancestors in the seventeenth
century. We cannot understand how it was possible for brilliant men to gather in Philadelphia and to declare that all men
are created equal, when some of them owned other men as
chattels. But soon some recognition of the inconsistency of
the position concerning equality began to enter men's consciousness, and when it did so, it came, in large measure, as a
result of what had occurred in Palestine centuries before.

Of all of the philosophers of the twentieth century, it now seems likely that Alfred North Whitehead will be remembered longest. The one Whitehead production that is almost sure to be remembered is *Adventures of Ideas*. In this remarkable book, the author has helped many sensitive readers to see that ideas have histories and that, though they unfold slowly, they can finally be effective in changing civilization. Slavery was finally undermined as an institution by ideas that did not come to flower for at least eighteen hundred years. Whitehead, because he was a great philosopher, was more than a philosopher. Something of his breadth is exhibited by the fact that the two sets of Lowell Lectures by which he made his debut into American intellectual life were first on science and then on religion.[6] He was interested in great ideas regardless of how they were classified.

In *Adventures of Ideas,* Professor Whitehead, while expressing great respect for the philosophers of the ancient world, made it clear that religion lends a driving force to philosophy. Thus, early Christianity provided something of extreme value that the venerable schools of philosophy had not been able to provide. Primitive Christians combined fierce enthusiasm with general ideas about the inherent dignity of the individual soul. Whitehead recognized the recovery of both of these features by the Methodists eighteen centuries later.

In an age of aristocracy in England, the Methodists appealed to the direct intuition of working men and of retail traders concerned with working men. In America they appealed to the toiling isolated groups of pioneers. They brought hope, fear, emotional release,

---

[6] The published books are *Science and the Modern World* (New York: The Macmillan Company, 1925) and *Religion in the Making* (New York: The Macmillan Company, 1926).

spiritual insight. They stemmed the inroads of revolutionary ideas. Also, allowing for many qualifications, they must be credited with one supreme achievement. They made the conception of the brotherhood of man and of the importance of men, a vivid reality. They had produced the final effective force which hereafter made slavery impossible among progressive races.[7]

The evangelicalism of the Methodists and their close associates produced, said Whitehead, "the final wave of popular feeling which drove the anti-slavery movement to success," but this does not mean that they were the originating force. "Neither the Catholics, nor the Methodists," the philosopher reported, "gave the first modern formulation of an explicit purpose to procure the abolition of slavery. This supreme honour belongs to the Quakers, and in particular to that Apostle of Human Freedom, John Woolman."[8]

The long story of the way in which the forces of the Christian faith, though operating slowly, finally made a difference in how men lived, should give us, if we are willing to observe it, a practical hint about the problems that we face at the end of the twentieth century. Many, it is true, talk glibly of the sacredness of persons, and this includes several who have no conscious adherence to the faith of Christ, but it is quite possible that without a religious anchorage, the doctrine of inherent human sacredness cannot be maintained. The forces of impersonalism, we must remember, are very strong. The deepest roots of what we call democracy are not to be found in ancient Greece, where democarcy experienced one of its greatest failures. It was, after all, the Athenian democracy that

[7] *Adventures of Ideas* (New York: The Macmillan Company, 1933), p. 28.
[8] *Ibid.*, pp. 28, 29.

pronounced the death sentence upon Socrates, "concerning whom I may truly say," said Plato, "that of all the men of his time whom I have known, he was the wisest and justest and best."[9] The deepest roots of democracy are found in the Bible, particularly in the revolutionary story of Naboth's Vineyard, in which both king and commoner stand on exactly the same level because both derive from the Divine paternity.

Whether the dignity of the individual, which lies at the heart of the entire struggle for equal rights and social justice, can be maintained permanently on any other basis we cannot know, but we shall, if we wish to be realistic, pay careful attention to the one basis that is known to be an effective place to stand, and from which many loads may be lifted. When we realize, with Whitehead and other historians of ideas, the way in which a free society traces its roots back to a religious belief and commitment, we shall not lightly neglect this revelation of how emancipation comes. Contemporary thinkers can profit from a new study of a striking essay, "The Free Society and Individual Rights," written by Theodore O. Wedel.[10] Canon Wedel was at great pains, in this essay, to show that the doctrine of the worth of every man is fundamentally derivative, rather than "a truth standing on its own." The needy neighbor may, in fact, be an unlovely person and might, in a purely secular society, reasonably be liquidated to the profit of the state. The most notorious of Roman dictators operated unashamedly on this basis, but Christianity, with all its mistakes, took a different tack.

"The dogma of individual rights," wrote Wedel, "is not a truth standing on its own. It is a derivative dogma and depends

[9] *Phaedo*, 118A.
[10] Printed as the first essay in *The Christian Demand for Social Justice*, edited by Bishop William Scarlett (New York: A Signet Special, 1949).

upon divine, not secular sanctions. It does not derive from a doctrine of the inherent goodness of *human nature*, or a sacredness of personality which man has earned. It derives, rather, from the doctrine of the sinfulness of human nature and the universal judgment and grace of a righteous God."[11] Here is a profound and exciting idea. If every man, in spite of his personal ineptitude, is God's handiwork, and if every man, including the leader or the king, is under judgment, we have a powerful motive for the creation of a social order in which there is maximum chance for equality of opportunity as well as equal justice. No one is outside the law, just as no one is outside the Divine Concern.

Such an understanding of the nature of the human situation provides a far stronger motive for overcoming racial injustice than does any merely economic or political or legal conception. If it could be followed with any sincerity, it would provide an antidote to all racism, whether of the white or the black variety. General acceptance of such convictions would not make laws unnecessary, but it would lead to the enactment of laws and, furthermore, help to provide some of the spirit that keeps men from circumventing laws by their own clever devices. A world in which men of different races can look upon men of contrasting color as Children of God is one in which equal freedom can come without bitterness.

We cannot say too often that Christianity is the most revolutionary of faiths, far more revolutionary, indeed, than any known form of communism, whether Marxist or Maoist. Contemporary schools of communism claim to be revolutionary, but they are not thoroughly so. They may decide to distribute property and thereby aid the dispossessed, but there is nothing,

[11] *Ibid.*, p. 15.

in any of their systems, about compassion for the person from whom the property is to be taken. He is a hated imperialist, and that is enough to say about him. But the Christian, if he understands his Lord, goes further. He is, of course, eager to help the poor, but he is not willing to settle for hatred or contempt for the original owner, since the owner, too, like the landless, is an unconditional object of Divine Concern. We need to work in all known ways to see that the Negro in America is given a chance to earn a decent living, to enjoy equal schooling, and to inhabit equal housing, but underneath all of these forms of equality is that of equal respect. This is what every man desires, and the most powerful motivation for giving it is that provided by the Gospel of Christ. We do well to insist upon voting rights, but if we end there, the battle has only begun. We are never far on the way until the white man sees the black, not only as an equal politically, but spiritually as a brother.

Any honest observer is bound to admit that some of the worst examples of oppression have occurred in areas in which the Gospel has been preached and believed. But while this is true, it is only part of the truth. The other, and the more important part, is that the most encouraging changes in the southern part of the United States, in regard to race relations, are coming from primarily religious motives. Anyone who spends much time in southern states can hardly fail to notice the role of Christians in the effort to solve the problem that is so deep-seated and that has been with us so long.[12] Wherever the Bible is honored there is real hope, because the Bible clearly teaches that all mankind is of one family.

---

[12] For a careful estimate of this, written by one born in the South, see Kyle Haselden, *Morality and the Mass Media* (Nashville: The Broadman Press, 1968), p. 68.

Another valuable teaching, which needs to be remembered when we are working to bring about a better social order, is that we shall never have perfection in the relations between human beings. Much of the frustrated anger of our time results from utterly naïve expectations that are inevitably unfulfilled. The Christian faith, when understood, helps to avoid the bitterness of disillusionment by making it clear in advance that there will be no Utopia. The impossibility of Utopia follows logically from the chronic character of human sin, which infects the planners in the same way that it infects those for whom the new social order is planned. The experience of ideal communities in America is pathetically uniform, and the sad truth is that each *fails*.

We shall avoid much bitterness and idle recrimination if we realize in advance that there is a wide difference between the degree of perfection possible in an individual and in a society. There was, for example, much more that was admirable about the character of William Penn than there was about the "Holy Experiment" that he sought to execute in the new world. Though his experiment had some good features, it was, in considerable measure, a failure, as is bound to be true with anything that has people in it.

It is inevitable that there should be a radical difference between what we are considering in this chapter and what was considered in Chapter III. The personal life, particularly in its solitude, can often attain a high degree of excellence. It is more nearly possible, in short, to learn to pray well than it is to serve well, because, though some prayer involves others, all service involves others, and that is where the trouble begins. A man has made a few steps on the road to wisdom if he knows the difference between the two complementary realms. The door to life represented by "we" opens more widely than does the door represented by "I," but it is harder to keep it open.

There are two forms of foolishness to be avoided assiduously in this connection. It is equally foolish either to entertain Utopian hopes or to abandon the struggle because of lack of perfect accomplishment. Perfectionism is evil because it often causes people to give up when they learn that the ideal commonwealth cannot be established on the banks of the Wabash or anywhere else.[13] Perfectionism is always harmful when the abstract best becomes the enemy of the concrete good. The intelligent procedure is to understand that the ideal will not be achieved and then to try, with all our might, to make the situation relatively better than what it was before. We shall not experience a perfect social order, either now or a thousand years from now, but some improvement is possible, and this is what keeps thoughtful men going.

The person who sincerely desires to serve his fellow men soon finds that the service side of his life, far from standing alone, requires not only a deep inner life of devotion, but also the third leg of our stool, the life of critical intelligence. Without careful thought, the individual may easily find himself upholding positions that once made sense, but do so no more, because the battle front changes. A good many people are still fighting old battles on the supposition that the major danger is still what it formerly was. It is part of our needed realism now—a realism in which committed Christians should take the lead—to point out that we are in a new day in which the major danger, which once came from the right, now comes from the left.

---

[13] Two famous Utopian experiments, that of the Rappites and that of Robert Owen, were conducted at New Harmony, Indiana.

Without vigilant examination of what we are doing, it is easy to evince more interest in causes or in dogmas than in persons. It is not uncommon, for instance, for white crusaders, deeply committed to civil rights, to have no close friends or even acquaintances among black people, but social action cannot meet the test of authenticity unless it is profoundly personal. Careful intellectual attention may likewise save us from the mistake of supposing that others who do not share our particular solutions of social problems are less concerned with social action than we are.

Almost everyone has heard some public speaker deplore the obvious gap between what we do technologically and what we do socially. If we would only put as much disciplined intelligence and money into psychology or sociology as we now put into physics and chemistry, it is asserted, we should do as well with the social order as we have done with landing men on the moon. This popular judgment reveals a pathetic fallacy. We are dealing with problems of a radically different character when we deal with persons rather than with things. It is possible to achieve striking success in producing a rocket, since we are dealing with essentially passive materials that do not exercise freedom of decision and do not sin. But people, by contrast, cannot be manipulated as physical objects can be, and we are glad that this is true. The study of psychology is worth pursuing, but it is naïve to suppose that such study will bring to human society the kind of success possible in a scientific laboratory. Scientists, it should be carefully noted, find it far easier to manipulate their environment than to manage themselves.

The much-publicized gap between scientific success and success with human life is not surprising to anyone who understands something of the Christian faith. We must use all of the intelligence that we can muster in the organization of human behavior, for emotion will not suffice, but even when we do so, there will be disappointments at every level. We must build colleges, but colleges will be centers of dissension; we must support labor unions, but unions will be involved in power struggles; we must have a movement for civil rights, but the movement will be exploited by demagogues; we must administer welfare, but there will be corruption in its administration. Only the realist can operate without debilitating discouragement.

We need to give careful attention today to the relationship between social service and evangelism. The danger is that service may take the place of evangelism or that evangelism may be redefined so that it is social service and nothing more. However desirable it may be to help workers to organize or even, in extreme instances, to strike, this does not and cannot take the place of evangelism in the sense of confrontation with Jesus Christ. The more deeply involved a person comes to be in the Christian Cause, the more he will reject simplistic approaches, and the reduction of evangelism to social action is such an approach. The early injunction of Christ was to become "fishers of men" (Mark 1:17), and this is quite as significant as the injunction to feed the hungry. To feed a man is important; but man does not live by bread alone, so it is equally important to make him sense the love of Christ. If we do only the one and not the other we may, in the end, undermine the motivation even for the feeding itself. It is a serious mistake to seek to change the environment without also changing the man.

The people who think that evangelism is dead or is fully

incorporated in acts of justice and mercy would do well to think again. How is the fire of social sensitivity to be sustained and replenished? The Christian is a man who, regardless of the century in which he lives, knows the answer; he knows that the way to become ignited is to approach the Source. "Whoever is near to me," said Christ, "is near to the fire."[14]

[14] *The Gospel According to Thomas* (New York: Harper & Row, 1959), p. 45.

V

Intellectual Integrity

The faith is an anvil which has worn out many hammers.

LORD TWEEDSMUIR

THOUGH PARADOX is always part of human life, the paradox of contemporary existence is extreme. We have achieved greatly, and some of our achievements have made us proud, and rightly so. The most striking of these are in the area of technology, culminating, for the present, in actually placing men on a celestial body, but we have also had some remarkable successes

105

in the social order. With these we are never satisfied, and we ought not to be satisfied, but if we are realistic, we admit that great strides have been made in overcoming poverty and hunger. That there is further to go need not lead us to deny the distance already traveled. A sense of history is helpful.

Central to the paradox is the fact that in spite of obvious successes there is an obvious lack of happiness. Happiness did, indeed, appear at the time of the first moon landing; but since the deep malaise remains, it was only temporary. On every side the manifest lack of laughter is so great that we may, not inaccurately, be termed the unlaughing generation. The plight of the theater is only one of many evidences of this. Nakedness, whatever else it is, is not funny. One objective measure of our unhappiness is found in the number of individuals who in desperation turn to drugs. Nor is the problem merely economic; many of the most unhappy faces belong to those who have plenty of money to spend. The association of unhappiness and affluence requires the most careful analysis.

We are making a real advance when we begin to recognize that much of the unhappiness in human life is caused by ideas. Many of these ideas seem new because they have recently become fashionable. The idea that "all is permitted" was exposed by Dostoevski in *The Brothers Karamazov*, but many today are not aware of either its philosophic roots or its logical consequences. The idea arises from the belief that there is really no objective moral right and that, consequently, there is no reason for action other than the changing desires of the individual. On this basis there is, of course, no reason why one man should not defraud another or even kill another, providing that is what he happens to want. If subjectivism in ethics is a sound philosophy, i.e., if there is no objective moral order in reference to which the act of the individual is right or wrong, then complete permissiveness is reasonable. If I believe that there is no objective moral order, I have no rational justification for objecting, on moral grounds, to anything that any man chooses to do to me. I may be able to strike him, or to shout at him, but I cannot rationally enter into dialogue with him, because, according to our premise, there is nothing to talk about. If subjectivism is accepted, the other man's desire to harm me is the end of the story, so far as rational discourse is concerned.

Much of the current malaise is the result of a lack of integrity, in the strict sense of that term. The problem is that many of the people who, on the one hand, are devoted to permissiveness, are also devoted, on the other hand, to social justice. Frequently, the very ones who practice sexual promiscuity, because they have rejected the whole idea of a moral law, are also the people who are most aroused by the alleged injustice of the military draft. But how can these go together? The truth is that they cannot go together because they are completely incompatible ideas. The resulting tension is bound to be harmful. If all is permitted, then why isn't injustice permitted? Indeed, how can injustice on this basis have any meaning at all?

If we propose to operate on the basis of ethical subjectivism, we have no right to claim that anything, anywhere, is really wrong. The systematic tolerance that recognizes both "your truth" and "my truth" leaves no room for dialogue. Why shouldn't the slave owner reply to Woolman's approach by the answer, "I like it this way?" The consistent subjectivist can have no further reply. What was to keep Hitler from claiming that persecution of the Jews was *his* truth? But if rational dialogue is logically impossible, what then? All that remains is the capacity to shout the other fellow down, or to hit him over the head with a chair, and this, in fact, is what occurs. Violence is inevitable if reason is undermined.

The wide acceptance of the philosophy of subjective reference, often called relativism, has been accelerated by many features of our age. For instance, the ease of travel, which technology makes possible, allows thousands to develop some acquaintance with cultures other than their own. Almost everyone, as a result, is now aware that what is considered beautiful by some is considered ugly by others. One set of people thinks communism is the hope of mankind while another set thinks it is not. Consequently, many jump to the conclusion that beauty exists only in the eye of the beholder and that, similarly, ideas of right and wrong are relative only to what the individual thinks. Some people, according to this logic, approve of white supremacy and some don't, and they are both right. Tolerance of this sort leads rationally to indifference, but the odd circumstance is that so few are willing to accept the logical consequence. While we demand tolerance of our own acts, we are violently intolerant of the acts of others. Such a lack of intellectual integrity is bound to be destructive of persons. It is the chief mark of intellectual honesty that a man will not accept any proposition unless he is also willing to accept the implications of that position.

The contemporary Christian is called to operate against the background of the paradox of unhappiness. His vocation is to understand the causes of the confusion and to provide an acceptable alternative to it. His task is to try to roll back the tide that, in spite of technological success, threatens to engulf mankind. Since a people in whom the self-contradiction of ideas becomes general will decay, no matter how brilliant it may be in other ways, the time may easily come when even the technological successes will be no longer possible. What if the astronauts were as confused as many of their compatriots?

The new man who will be able to provide leadership in our confused and confusing time must be a true intellectual, in the sense that he is a rationalist. The Christian intellectual will be concerned, not primarily with church politics, but with the world, because he knows that it is the function of the church to change the mood of the world. There are available to him important resources for his task, because Christianity, in all of its great periods, has been conspicuously rational. The Christian, if he understands his faith, is the genuine radical of his generation in that he is willing and able to challenge the widely accepted assumption that truth is only relative to one's self and one's wishes.

In loyalty to his heritage, the Christian thinker will challenge popular antirationalism wherever he finds it. Sometimes he must work almost alone in this essentially philosophical task, for there are universities in which philosophy, as normally understood in the past, is not even attempted now. In his aloneness, the Christian must be sufficiently tough-minded to see that if reason is discarded, and if two contradictory positions can be held at the same time, the human search for excellence is at an end. A world in which anything goes will ultimately be a world in which nothing goes. If we give up reason, why should we prefer the wisdom of Blaise Pascal to the wisdom of Timothy Leary?

Much of our trouble has come because so many Christian teachers have not recognized the necessity of noting and combating a false set of presuppositions. There are presuppositions so important that, if they are allowed to stand, the battle is already lost. If we accept the assumption that there is no objective truth about morality, we are already boxed into a position in which we cannot even discuss sin, for there is no value in analyzing individual sins if the very idea is meaningless. We lose the battle, not when the confrontation occurs, but much farther back.

After a long period in which it has been fashionable to minimize, even in Christian circles, the importance of belief, we may be ready now for a radical change. It has been commonly said that it is what people do that matters most, but we have frequently neglected the further observation that what people believe determines, in large measure, what they do. It may be better to worship God than to believe in Him, but if we do not have the latter we shall not long have the former. "How are men to call upon him in whom they have not believed?" (Rom. 10:14). It may be better to serve our fellow men than to give assent to a creed, but the deeper consideration is that the way in which we treat other people depends ultimately upon what we believe about them. If we believe that persons are only forked radishes, of complex structure, there is no good reason to value them or to seek to liberate them from various kinds of bondage, but if, by contrast, we believe that they are persons for whom Christ died, we are bound to look upon all men and women, regardless of their unattractiveness, with respect.

It is because of the importance of objective belief that the Christian must seek to avoid sentimentality. It is a mark of sentimentality to suppose that we can keep the fruits of our religion when the roots are allowed to wither. The antisentimentalist does not flinch in the face of hard choices. He knows that when there is a clear contradiction, he cannot have it both ways. For example, if Christ did not rise, then it is simple honesty to say frankly that those who thought that He rose were deluded. It is strange to see how many of the people of our time are unwilling to face such an unhappy consequence.

A test case of intellectual tough-mindedness is prayer. A commonly held position is that of people who hesitate to give up prayer completely, even though they have rejected the philosophy that makes genuine prayer intelligible. One does not need to be a deep thinker to sense the radical difference between prayer and autosuggestion, but if God does not exist, as so many people apparently believe, autosuggestion is all that remains possible. If God does not exist, in fact, then we may as well give up both prayer and miracle, as well as any confidence in the survival of consciousness after the death of the body. If God is *not*, then all worship, in which so many persons of different ages and different cultures have engaged, is a fraud and a hoax. What is left is meditation, but that is a different matter entirely.

The Christian who wishes to be truly modern will have to pay the price of rigorous thinking, for cheap modernity is transparently ineffective and really deludes nobody. Does anyone really believe that the gospel is better received if its presentation is accompanied by the use of a guitar? If contemporary prophets wish to make their maximum contribution to the improvement of society, they should try to deal, not with organizational tricks, but with exciting truth. People certainly don't respond affirmatively when they are directed to religion, but sometimes they respond powerfully when they are directed to God. Men are not brought into Christ's orbit, ordinarily, by being recruited as ushers, but only by becoming deeply convinced of Christ's truth. The hope lies, not in new activities, but in new convictions. We have seen some new men, who now shock their relatives and fellow church members because they really believe that Christ is the center of their lives. Often one such person has more effect than is provided by the activity of *a hundred nominal members.*

It is a blessing that we have thousands of dedicated pastors, but their existence is not sufficient if they do not apply their energies where they are needed most. The pastors can make a tremendous difference in our civilization if they cease to be operators of clubs and become arousers of conviction. In the modern scene every Christian pastor should be primarily an evangelist, not only because of the world outside, but also because of the members, who constitute, in themselves, a mission field. The new strategy is to convince and then to equip, but they must be convinced *first.*

We must recognize that we are in an essentially new situation, one in which millions of our people literally have never heard the great ideas of Basic Christianity. In a former generation, many replied, "Oh, that is what I heard when I was little," but few can honestly say that now, for the fact is that they have not heard. There are millions of our contemporaries who have never even entertained the exciting idea that the central power of the universe is not some material that decays, not some energy that inevitably dissipates, not some law that is impersonal and abstract, but Infinite Personal Mind. Most have never heard the excellent reasons for believing that theism is objectively true, and is therefore not merely a projection of human wishes or hopes or illusions. They have not been confronted with the powerful cumulative evidence that includes an understanding of science, the life of reason, and the reports of direct religious experience.

One of the most surprising weaknesses of the Christian ministry in the recent past has been the neglect of rigorous theology. Preachers, assuming what they had no right to assume, have dealt in their sermons with peripheral topics, without realizing that many of the members are lacking in the fundamentals. What good is it to talk about God's will for our social crisis to people who do not really believe in Him? The residue is an essentially impotent humanism that finally leads to despair once self-sufficiency crumbles, as it will. Idealization of humanity is a very poor substitute for faith in the Living God, because it is a fact that other humans disappoint us. If all that we have is faith in something called religion, it turns out to be a pathetic substitute for faith in the God who is, who was, and who will be. We ought to pay attention to the fact that in spite of the apparently dominant humanism, many people turn, in genuine crises, to the great affirmations. This is especially obvious in the crucial experience of the death of a loved one. Indeed, there is more dissatisfaction with meaningless living, and with hopeless death, than has appeared to be the case. There is real significance in the fact that nearly all Americans, with the exception of the dedicated atheists, seem to have been glad when the astronauts, circling near the moon at Christmas time, 1968, read the early verses of Genesis. Such a response shows that there is a deeper dissatisfaction with confusion and with superficiality than we have ordinarily supposed existed. Christian leaders, if they are wise, will make their contribution accordingly.

Christian teachers who dwell on the "difficulties" of such doctrines as the Virgin Birth and the Fall of Man are out of touch with the climate of opinion of their pupils. The new situation is not that of difficulty at the periphery, but rejection at the center. Why bother to trim the branches if the root is dead? There is a clear hunger in modern life for attention to the central issues. God is or is not; what is the evidence? Humans survive death or they do not; what have we a right to believe? In all such discussion the committed Christian must be sure to make clear that the question is never that of what we *want* to believe, for it is better to face the uncomforting truth than to accept the comforting falsehood. If Christianity is not true, then it is a manifest evil that honest people will abandon, whatever the consequences.

How do we know the truth? Never does it come to us in a simplistic fashion, but always by the method of comparative difficulties. The Christian teacher, because he is aware of difficulties in connection with the existence of God or the Life Everlasting, is careful not to deny such difficulties. What he does, instead, is to face also the difficulties of any alternative position. There are, indeed, problems that make theism hard to accept, particularly that concerning the amount of unproductive suffering in the world which seems to be inconsistent with belief in God's loving care, but the honest thinker does not end there. He examines likewise the difficulties of atheism and often finds them to be far greater than are the difficulties of theism. For example, the atheist knows that the world includes self-conscious persons, because it includes him, but he has an insurmountable difficulty when he tries to believe that personality, such as he demonstrates, has arisen in a fundamentally impersonal world. He is placed in the unenviable position of concluding that the principle of sufficient reason does not operate, because he thinks that what is unconscious has produced consciousness, and that what has no moral significance has produced goodness.

A modern author has called the idea that personality could arise out of an impersonal world an example of metaphysical magic. "No one," he says, "has presented an idea, let alone demonstrated, how it is feasible to explain how the impersonal beginning, plus chance, can give personality."[1] It is the duty of Christian teachers to expose and to oppose magic wherever it appears. The Christian must avoid the impression of seeming to uphold just any faith. One way in which he can earn a reputation for beneficent skepticism is to help people to see the essential credulity of many of their nonreligious ideas. This may not, in all cases, bring men to Christ, but it may take away some of the intellectual barriers to full commitment to Him. The Christian teacher is rendering a genuine service when he helps to set men free from dependence upon what is fundamental nonsense, for it is the truth that sets men free.

The Christian thinker must help people to see the inadequacy of positions which they adopt in their desperation, but which may serve only to deepen the confusion. One such position is pantheism. There has been a great deal of vague pantheism in our generation, even though it is seldom called by that name. We always have some degree of pantheism whenever we reject God's separate existence and refer only to the Divine immanence in the world. A great deal of what was, until yesterday, called the "new theology" was tinged with this character. It has naturally been perplexing to ordinary people, and especially to those who are conscious Christians, because

[1] Francis A. Schaeffer, *The God Who is There* (Chicago: Inter-Varsity Press, 1968), p. 88.

this theology has employed some of the evangelical language, but has meant something else by it.

If the Christian thinker is sufficiently alert, he will not be impressed by rejection of "God out there," when what this really means is rejection of the whole idea of God as independent of the world that He has made. A God who would cease with the end of our physical system, as the God of all pantheism would, cannot be mentioned intelligibly along with the God of Abraham, of Isaac, and of Jacob. God, as revealed in the Bible, is not equated with all that is, because He is prior to all else than Himself, and can survive the end of the world. The deepest error of pantheism is that, if God is all that is, then He includes sin and evil, and thus is not even remotely similar to the Father of Jesus Christ. The God of pantheism, being beyond good and evil, makes the struggle against evil essentially meaningless. Why should we care about injustice if God does not? The difficulty with pantheism, in either its ancient or modern form, is not that it is too intellectual, but that it is not intellectual enough.

As we try to meet the conditions for the restoration of meaning in human thought, we must be very clear about the question of existence. Because it has been fashionable in the recent past even for theologians to deny that God exists, we must help people to overcome confusion on this subject. The theologian who denies Divine existence is not meaning to say that God is not at all, but rather that He is beyond the category of existence with its supposed limitations. High-minded as this intention has been, we must honestly report that it has been both an intellectual and a spiritual failure. Certainly it has confused many readers, and part of the reason is that the writers have themselves often been confused. Fortunately, there is now available a considerable body of scholarly yet profoundly devout published thinking that again helps to make the idea of Divine existence intellectually respectable.[2]

A Christian is one who believes that God exists just as truly as a stone exists. The fact that God is utterly different from the stone has no bearing on whether the object of our awareness is genuine or imaginary. The real alternative to existence is what is *imagined*, and if God is an imaginary Being, we may as well cease to engage in all talk about Him. The intelligent operation, then, would be to forget the subject and to go on with something pertinent to our lives. We must be sufficiently unsentimental to admit that what is nonexistent is only delusory, for that which does not exist has only subjective reference. A God who has only subjective reference, who is only an idea and not a genuine Being, is far indeed from the One to whom Christ prayed as "Lord of heaven and earth" (Matt. 11:25).

The Christian faith cannot perform a redemptive role in the modern world unless it gives strong leadership on the central issues of faith. If the members of the church are primarily concerned with erecting a new building or buying a new piano or new choir robes, they will not even begin to meet the need that modern seekers so deeply feel. Because the confusion of minds has been great, and because some of it has been caused by Christian leaders, what is required is a sharp alteration of strategy so that we engage in the ministry of clarification. We must reverse the conventional procedure, and begin with Christ. Then we come to know God as a consequence of our faith in Christ. It might be helpful to modern men and women

[2] See Helmut Gollwitzer, *The Existence of God as Confessed by Faith* (Philadelphia: Westminster Press, 1965).

to change the order of items in the classic creeds so that a believer can say, "I believe in Jesus Christ, and consequently I believe in the One whom He reveals, the Lord God Almighty."

If our initial certitude is the reliability and trustworthiness of Christ, we cannot, with intellectual honesty, fail to go on to worship the Father, because Christ worshiped Him. In short, the man who calls himself a Christian atheist is simply a confused individual, who does not follow the logic of his own position.

The being of God is very hard for modern man to accept. Unless he thinks with unusual care, he is tempted to think of God as a mere idea or as an abstraction. That is why it is strategically a mistake to begin with God, whom no man has seen at any time. There is real danger that the whole conception may be so vague as to be practically meaningless. But Christ is not vague at all. He lived on earth; He lives now; and He draws us to the magnificent conclusion that the God of all the world and of mankind is really like Him. Though it is still true, then, that no man at any time has *seen* God, it is likewise true that Christ has revealed Him (John 1:18). The most exciting doctrine of the Christian faith is not the divinity of Christ, but the Christlikeness of God. The hope is that this is something that modern man can both understand and appreciate.

Important as the question of God's existence may be, the question of His nature is equally important. God might exist and yet be malicious or vengeful; He might not be concerned with persons like ourselves; He might be no more than a Ground of Being or even an abstraction; He might be as impersonal as a Force or a law of nature. If any of these were true conceptions, the awareness of God's existence would not provide an antidote to human futility, but might accentuate it. The Good News, by contrast, a kind of news that can over-come a sense of lostness, is that God not only is, but that God, being like Christ, cares personally for every one of His crea-tures. If all of the rest of Christ's teaching were lost, we could still be lifted by the tremendous affirmation that the Lord of heaven and earth is concerned with the fall of the sparrow (Luke 12:6). He is like the shepherd who goes out to seek the *one* that is lost (Luke 15:3-7).

Modern man can be helped immeasurably by the realization that at the heart of all that is, stands not mere power, but *A Person*. We have all been aware of the temptation to think of God in impersonal terms, on the mistaken assumption that this has somehow liberated us from childish superstition or, when we want to sound impressive, from what we call "an-thropomorphism." The odd consequence is that in this under-standable effort, we have moved down rather than up; a force is clearly inferior to a person, since a person can know a force while a force cannot know either a person or itself. A person is not a being with a body, though we, as finite persons, happen now to inhabit bodies. A person is any being, finite or infinite, capable of reflective thought, of self-consciousness, and of caring. The greatest of these is caring.

We are given a keen sense of the need of more rigorous thought on the deepest questions when we encounter persons who are trying to hold on to some idea of God, but who, at the same time, reject the personal relationship that Christ taught and illustrated. It is not uncommon to hear someone say, "I cannot believe in a personal God, but I believe in a dynamic force behind the universe." The first important thing to say about this is that it is a very peculiar position, so peculiar, in fact, that it is not easy to see how any thoughtful person can maintain it. In some ways, outright atheism would be preferable, because it would at least be less confused. It is possible to understand or even to appreciate the forthright atheist, since he certainly has some evidence on his side, but there is very little to be said for a person who supposes that a Force is superior to a Person as a Source of ultimate causation.

There is no use in talking of the existence of God at all unless we mean, when we use the word, something logically prior to the created order, and also something that is *not inferior* to the products of that order. Man, who is one of the products, is both conscious and self-conscious. If God is only a Force, and cannot be referred to in fully personal terms, He is clearly inferior to that class of products which we represent. The important task is that of helping people to see how odd it would be for God to lack what even the most modest of men are able to enjoy. *We* can know and care, and if God cannot, He is inferior to us. The absurdity of this is too great to be acceptable to anyone when once he sees it clearly. The ultimate explanation of the wonder and mystery of the universe, which keeps it from being merely mysterious, must be something that transcends what is derivative from it, and is at least equal in value to the noblest of the derivatives. There is no use in believing in God unless we understand that what is ultimate has about it those qualities of rationality, purpose, and compassion in which human beings glory. What is amazingly irrational is that human beings, who value personal qualities more than they value forces, should count it an improvement to describe God by employing a metaphor drawn from physics rather than one drawn from the experiences of love and affection.

It is important to make an effort to understand the meaning

of the pronoun "Thou." Though we have largely lost this valuable little word in everyday conversation, the brilliant thinking of the famous Jewish philosopher, Martin Buber, has restored some of the wonder of the "I-Thou" relationship. As soon as we think about it at all, we can see the radical difference between the "I-Thou" relationship and the contrasting relationship expressed by "I-it." Whatever is an "it," Buber taught us, is something that with impunity we can use as a tool, but the relationship to a "thou" is different in kind. It is significant that "thou" is intrinsically singular while "you" is not. "You" can be used, and is used, in addressing a crowd in which the persons are not known, but anyone who says "thou," and says it meaningfully, is well aware that he is speaking only to *one*.

The important observation for those who take their faith seriously is that the word "thou" is one of the most valuable words of the entire Biblical heritage. The deeper the Psalms become, the more personal they are, and the evidence of this is in the use of the second person singular. God is not One who is discussed or argued about, but One who is encountered. It is striking to discover the growth in this direction in the Psalm that many love best, the twenty-third. In this supreme classic of devotion, God is, at first, the One who is spoken about. "He maketh me to lie down in green pastures." But the mood changes abruptly in the fourth verse, when the reverent one says, "Yea, though I walk through the valley of the shadow of death, I will fear no evil: for thou art with me." Though this is one of the most radical changes that can be imagined, many have been so familiar with the beautiful words that they have never noticed it. What it means is that at the profoundest depths men talk not *about* God but *with* Him.

The example of the Shepherd Psalm does not stand alone. It is almost impossible, for example, to miss the profound significance of the words, "O Lord, thou hast searched me, and known me. Thou knowest my downsitting and mine uprising, thou understandest my thought afar off" (Ps. 139:1, 2, AV). It is a serious mistake for modern men and women to dismiss this as being merely Biblical language, thus failing to understand that it is clearly meant to be intensely personal language. Christ echoes this when He began His most personal prayer, "I thank *thee*" (Matt. 11:25).

An examination of the Biblical use of the language of direct intimacy offers a deeper understanding of what it means to be a *person*. A person is any being to whom the word "thou" or even "you" can be intelligibly addressed! No one ever says "thou" to a physical object or to a principle or to a law, but God, if Christ is right, is neither a physical object nor a principle nor a law. He is, instead, One who knows us perfectly and whom we can partly know. It is highly reasonable to conclude that the ultimate source of our world, which includes persons, is personal, because persons make things, while things do not make persons. One of the major mistakes of modern man, even when he has been reverent, is that his conception of God has been too small. The only conception big enough to account for the world that we know is that of Infinite Personal Mind. In some Eastern religions, God is seen as infinite, but not personal; in the religions of ancient Greece, the gods were envisaged as personal, but finite; in the Biblical heritage, God is both personal and infinite. Skeptics may be able to dismiss ceremonies and priesthood and sacred buildings, but the Eternal Thou is a different matter.

When we try desperately to be contemporary, we adapt

the faith to current modes of thought in the mistaken assumption that Christian ideas are thus made more palatable. But Christians make very little impact when they engage in this strategy, because they thereby provide no challenge. In its great periods, the Christian faith has been shocking to contemporaries, because it has challenged them by its refusal to conform. Christians must attack the world in its subjectivism, in its superficial humanism, and, above all, in its irrationalism. A great deal of contemporary Christian teaching, especially in sermons, has failed because it has not been sufficiently disturbing.

On all sides today we encounter the automatic dismissal of miracle. The miracles of Christ, as reported in the Gospels, are often explained naturalistically, the healings being assumed to be psychological and the feedings the result of sharing of provisions already on hand. The resurrection of Christ from the dead is denied, even by many church members, not because it is lacking in good historical evidence, which it is not, but because they say it *could not occur*. When we ask why it could not occur, the somewhat embarrassed answer is that such an event would be contrary to natural laws. But what is this, other than a naturalistic bias? Which is ultimate and primary, the laws of nature or their Creator and Sustainer? Because this is a question that millions have never even entertained, it is the task of thoughtful Christians to raise it.

In those areas in which the exponents of the Gospel now receive a hearing, the most welcome voices are those that uphold a supernatural view of reality without any apology. The differences between the denominations are not exciting to anybody, and even the old controversy between fundamentalists and modernists is obviously out of date. The issue between naturalism and supernaturalism, however, has an appeal to the modern mind, because the issue is crucial. One of the clearest of Christian spokesmen, Harry Blamires, was enough ahead of his time to see the emergence of the new issue more than ten years ago. Study of contemporary thought, he wrote in 1956, "leads one to the conclusion that, in the near future, the dominating controversy within Christendom will be between those who give full weight to the supernatural reality at the heart of all Christian dogma, practice and thought, and those who try to convert Christianity into a naturalistic religion by whittling away the reality and comprehensiveness of its supernatural basis."[3]

Almost anyone can see that if the conventional naturalism is true, God's existence makes very little difference, for He is relegated by it to a minor role. He does not, on the naturalistic thesis, participate directly and immediately in the world that He has made, but is limited by its laws. Such a God is not interesting to anyone, and especially not to the person who recognizes his need of help because of the meaninglessness of his own life.

Those who deny the supernatural are also obliged, in logical consistency, to deny transcendence. God, then, is limited to the world. Though it may seem odd, it is true that many who uncritically reject the conception of Divine transcendence do not go on to draw the necessary conclusion that the running down of the universe, as envisioned in the Second Law of Thermodynamics, will mean the end of God. If God is limited to the physical universe, the demise of the universe will be His demise, too. Whatever else we may say of this curious

[3] *The Faith and Modern Error* (New York: The Macmillan Company, 1956), p. 55.

notion, we can at least point out that it is diametrically opposed to the conception of God as found in both the Hebrew and Christian Scriptures. According to the Biblical faith, while the world is dependent upon God, God is neither dependent upon the world nor limited to it. His purpose involves our human welfare, but He may have other purposes of which we are unaware and which, in our finitude, we can neither understand nor appreciate. The authentic word of transcendence is as follows: "Before the mountains were brought forth, or ever thou hadst formed the earth and the world, even from everlasting to everlasting, thou art God" (Ps. 90:2, AV).

A thoroughgoing supernaturalism may be accepted by modern man, not because it provides comfort or emotional satisfaction, but because it makes more sense out of this mysterious world than does any alternative of which we know. Certainly it is not absurd. If modern man desires to be broad-minded, here is an answer to his quest. A world in which there are both nature and supernature exhibits a magnitude not offered by a world that is only natural. Supernaturalism accounts both for the orderliness of natural law, which is an exhibition of God's steady purpose, and for those occasions that we call miraculous, in which God's purpose is made unusually clear, because the unusual is required for the accomplishment of the Divine purpose. The world, then, is marked by order rather than by caprice, but the essence of the order is that of the Eternal Mind rather than unconscious law. If supernaturalism is true, as the Bible clearly teaches, natural law is neither primary nor autonomous, but is as truly derivative as is any other created thing. If natural law is derivative, it is subject to God's thought and is, therefore, not immutable. Miracle, then, is not a denial of rationality, but one of its chief expressions. If the rising of Christ from the dead was necessary for God's redemptive purpose for His world, then it was the most rational of events.

The Christian man who would be the genuinely new man that our age requires must gain new confidence. His may be a minority position, but this has occurred before, and the Christian witness has nevertheless survived. There are, of course, new dangers, but it is the vocation of Christians in every generation to outthink all opposition. There have always been predictions of the end of the Christian movement, but these predictions have been uniformly erroneous.

The faith is indeed an anvil that has worn out many hammers. The faith that could survive in spite of the condescension of the Greek thinkers, the fierce opposition of Roman emperors, the blight of the Dark Ages, and all the challenges of the modern world, is not likely to disappear in our time. Whatever contemporary analysts may say, this is not the post-Christian age. It may be the pre-Christian age, but that is another matter altogether.